THE TERRACOTTA DESIGNS OF

ALFRED WATERHOUSE

COLIN CUNNINGHAM

**THE NATURAL HISTORY MUSEUM, LONDON
IN ASSOCIATION WITH**

⊛WILEY-ACADEMY

For John Thackray

First published in Great Britain in 2001 by
WILEY-ACADEMY

A division of
JOHN WILEY & SONS
Baffins Lane
Chichester
West Sussex PO19 1UD
ISBN: 0 471 48949 2

Other Wiley Editorial Offices
New York, Weinheim, Brisbane, Singapore & Toronto

Design & Art Direction: Alun Evans & Kalina Owczarek

Printed and bound in Hong Kong

foreword

4   The Natural History Museum is a remarkable institution which not only brings natural history to millions of people who visit its exhibitions, but also serves as a major research organization. Behind the scenes scientists study the Museum's magnificent collections as well as carrying out biological and geological research internationally in order to increase our understanding of our natural world. Both the public and the scientific side of the Museum's work are housed in one of London's finest and best-loved buildings, created by the Museum's first superintendent Richard Owen, designed by the architect Alfred Waterhouse, and completed in 1881. Clad in terracotta, the building is truly a secular cathedral: a celebration of natural history.

Visitors will immediately be struck by the array of terracotta beasts confronting them as they approach the Museum. Inside the main entrance terracotta monkeys scramble up the arch in the central hall, and everywhere one looks one can see galleries adorned with terracotta fish, shells, birds, and many other creatures both from the present day and from the geological past. They epitomise the world that the Museum both studies and exhibits to the public. All of the mouldings were derived directly from drawings made by Waterhouse himself, and these drawings themselves form part of the Museum's very fine art collection. Although they are working drawings, created for a very practical purpose, they stand as distinctive and beautiful works of art in their own right. Once the terracotta moulds had been produced, the drawings were no longer needed for their immediate practical purpose, and so of the many hundreds that must have been created, large numbers have been lost. Fortunately, more than a hundred drawings have survived, which makes them all the more precious.

If you compare the drawings with the terracotta figures to which they gave rise, it is clear that the drawings show considerably more detail and delicacy. This is perhaps not surprising since the production of terracotta figures is a difficult process that relies on great accuracy to overcome the shrinkage that occurs during the firing process. In addition, of course, the drawings are two dimensional, and were used principally as a guide for Waterhouse's mould-maker to translate his ideas into three dimensions. It is a testament both to the skill of the mould-maker, M Dujardin, and to the faith that Waterhouse had in him, that the resulting terracotta figures are so successful.

The great museums of South Kensington were created in the nineteenth century to demonstrate how science, art and applied art can come together. Nothing could demonstrate this fusion more clearly than the terracotta designs of Alfred Waterhouse. This book brings these designs together for the first time, and I hope very much that they will bring interest and pleasure to a very wide audience.

Neil Chalmers, Director, The Natural History Museum

preface

The Natural History Museum is a building of endless fascination. It is impossible to visit it without being impressed by the power of the main spaces or by the richness and variety of the ornament, and each successive visit is likely to reveal new riches in the decoration. There is, it is true, an ongoing tension between the desire to display the continuing processes of natural science and the shapes and images of the nineteenth-century museum, fixed forever in terracotta. Yet the building is itself part of the developing history of natural science and, as such, worthy of study both by the casual visitor and the scientist curious to learn how the discipline has developed over the generations. Both the building and the display of science that continues to justify it are symptomatic of humanity's wonder at the world. The originators of this institution – its founder, Richard Owen, and its architect, Alfred Waterhouse – set out to present their understanding of that world, choosing to house the displays in a structure that reproduced much of the natural environment on its walls.

As the building approaches its 120th anniversary, the opportunity to present the surviving designs for that ornamental creation is one that allows us to celebrate both the scientific endeavour of the Museum over the last century and a half, and the high value put on this temple of learning when it was first conceived. The Museum was fortunate indeed to find an architect whose creative ingenuity matched the drive of its first Superintendent. I count it a privilege to have been asked to provide a text to accompany the publication of the designs for its terracotta ornament. These largely speak for themselves, but the story of their translation into clay is one that will delight the architectural historian. I hope it will also satisfy a curiosity among the scientific community and intrigue the general reader.

In preparing this manuscript, I have been helped by so many people that it is difficult to name them all. I wish to thank the colleagues who encouraged me to do the work, the staff in the various libraries I have consulted, and finally, but by no means least, the publishing division of The Natural History Museum and the editorial and production team of John Wiley & Sons. I would like to thank in particular John Thackray, who dreamed up the whole project, Tim Benton, Neil Bingham, Trudy Brannan, Geremy Butler, Sam Colinette, Carol Gokçe, and the staff of The Natural History Museum Library, Ruth Harman, Charles Hinde and the staff of the RIBA Drawings Collection, Ibstock Hathernware Ltd, Carol Krinsky, George McHardy, the Public Record Office in Kew, Annie Robinson, Manuel Sorrano, Annabel and Michael Stratton, Susan Tunick, Jessie Waterhouse, Prudence Waterhouse and Carla Yanni. I would also like to thank the following for confirming the modern scientific names for The Appendix: Per Ahlberg, Barry Clarke, Oliver Crimmen, Andy Currant, Jerry Hooker, Sandy Knapp, Angela Milner and Frank Steinheimer. (Unless otherwise indicated, copyright in the images lies with the author; copyright in the plates lies with The Natural History Museum).

I
introduction

In 1962, The Natural History Museum acquired a collection of pencil drawings of mammals, plants and a range of other species, both living and extinct, which now forms a significant part of the Library's outstanding collection of paintings and drawings. Many of these artworks are important as the only record of now extinct species. Others are meaningful as creative reactions by artists, and several are by painters significant in the Western canon. Yet even these cannot compare to the unique collection of pencil drawings that forms the subject of this book. All 135 are by one artist; they were drawings made not to record specimens, nor to react to the exotica of nature, but as designs of flora and fauna with which to ornament the Museum building itself. They are, therefore, not scientific descriptions in any true sense, but were made to bridge the gap between accurate depiction and components that could be effectively fabricated in clay. I have, therefore, felt free as a non-scientist to use generic names in my text with a freedom equal to that with which they were drawn by Alfred Waterhouse. His menagerie, however, though only partly identifiable, does represent a concept of natural history – the concept that was to identify the building as the first home for the natural history collections of The British Museum, establishing it as a leading scientific institution of the nineteenth century. A separate appendix lists the species as named by Waterhouse, together with their locations in the building, and, as far as possible, modern scientific names and common names. However, as they are nineteenth-century drawings and the ornament was for a typically Victorian building, we have retained throughout the text the names provided by Waterhouse or, more likely, the various keepers who advised him.

This remarkable collection of drawings was the generous gift of Michael Waterhouse, the architect's grandson. A generation after they arrived in the museum and almost a century and a quarter after they were made, it is at last possible to present them to a wider public. This volume reproduces every one of the drawings, setting them in the context of terracotta ornament in general and the devising of the decorative scheme of the Museum in particular. The images will well repay examination for their own sake as the work of a fine draughtsman and as imaginative combinations of pattern and naturalistic depiction. The drawings are also unique in function and a rare record of co-operation between architect, scientist and sculptor. Each of these had a contribution to make and this book tells the story of how these three men, Alfred Waterhouse (1830–1905), Richard Owen (1804–1892) and M Dujardin (fl.1866–78) conceived the ornamental scheme, and how the drawings were developed, passing from pencil sketch to finished building block.

The array of creatures and twining plants that form the most interesting part of the ornament should be seen alongside the abstract patterned blocks, shafts and bases, string courses and corbels and all the rhythms of blue and cream terracotta that are the essence of the building's character as a whole. But the story does not end there, for the terracotta of the structure is supplemented by ornamental ironwork, stained glass and painted decoration. These other media were part of the overall scheme from the start, and the story of their achievement also has its place in the tale. The painted ceilings, in particular, are outstanding examples of a type of decoration that rarely survives; these are also discussed and illustrated.

But it is the series of pencil drawings that really brings us into contact with the creative mind that made this building what it is – one of the finest and best-loved Victorian buildings of Britain, if not of the Western world.

1. Crab roundel in the mullion of a basement window of the west wing.

2. Half-inch scale details of the upper part of the south towers, showing how each terracotta block was individually detailed. The sheet was traced and sent to the manufacturers 19 March 1878. (Pencil and buff, pink, green and black washes, 76 x 56 cm. Courtesy of the British Architectural Library, Drawings Collection)

Each sheet bears one or more design and, in many cases, the sheets are annotated with instructions and dates, letters or numbers, to show that they are part of a series. The collection consists of some 136 pages,[1] most of them approximately the same size, which were bound together in two volumes and cover the years from 1874 to 1878: that is, from a year after work began until three years before the opening of the completed structure. It comes as something of a disappointment to learn that, as a record of the ornament, the collection is incomplete. It is missing, for instance, all the drawings for the small roundels that adorn the mullions of the basement windows (fig 1), as well as those for the delightful capitals to the mullions of the ground-floor windows. As it is mainly those from the lower levels that are absent, one might guess that the earliest drawings were not thought to be valuable once the blocks were manufactured. Their loss is a sad gap in the collection.

What is left nonetheless provides a rich feast of draughtsmanship. In addition, almost 300 other drawings for the building – which in turn will only be a fraction of the many designs, sheets of details and drawings for services and fittings that were made in the ten-year construction period – survive in the Royal Institute of British Architects' Collection (fig 2).[2] The chances of survival for any individual sheet were less than good. However, once the building began to rise, and its quality was appreciated, Waterhouse may well have begun storing his sketches separately, feeling that they had a particular value. The fact that they are all much smaller than his usual office drawings may also have helped preserve them, since they will almost certainly have been stored separately.[3]

Those that survive were bound in two volumes, evidently made up some time after the commission was completed, with each page neatly numbered.[4] The drawings were not arranged in a precise sequence either by location or by date. Indeed, in some cases, the page numbers run counter to the labelling of a group of designs. A completely logical sequence would in fact have been difficult, since many sheets bear drawings of different dates and some have designs for various parts of the building. They are, however, arranged broadly to reflect the locations of the ornament, and to understand these, one needs to be clear about the principal spaces of the Museum. As designed by Owen and Waterhouse, the Museum consisted of a central Index Museum, reached directly from the principal entrance and its hall beneath the flying stairway. To the rear was another hall designed as the Museum of British Natural History; between these two, at first floor level, was a Refreshment Room. The principal displays were in three floors of galleries along the south front, and the rear of the site was given over to a series of single-storey top-lit study galleries. These were alternately wide, for public access, and narrow, for student use, and were separated from the main galleries by a long transverse, or north, corridor. In addition, there was rich decoration for the façade, which consisted of east and west pavilions, central towers with the main entrance between them, and, on each side, the eleven identical bays of the display galleries. Finally, the scheme included a pair of porters' lodges and boundary wall with piers. All these elements were decorated with the terracotta creatures and patterns that Waterhouse designed.

In describing the drawings, I have retained the terms used by Waterhouse, to avoid confusion between the names of spaces and what is written on the drawing. It may be helpful here to set down the principal spaces as Waterhouse and Owen named them, together with their current titles. Externally, the building is much as Waterhouse designed it, apart from the destruction of one of the porters' lodges by a bomb during World War II.[5] Waterhouse's divisions of the façade into the central towers and principal entrance, flanked by east and west wings and their respective pavilions, remains the easily recognisable layout. The Entrance Hall is now generally regarded as part of the Central Hall, which is the title currently given to the Index Museum, intended to present a summary of world natural history. The Museum of British Natural History has become the North Hall or Waterhouse Café, and the original first-floor Refreshment Room is now the Plant Power exhibition. The principal display galleries on the ground and first floors of the nineteenth-century building retain their function, though they now have their own titles, but the second-floor galleries have been converted into offices. The long transverse corridor is still there, renamed Waterhouse Way. The rear galleries, however, have been much altered, now housing bookshops and rest rooms as well as a handful of exhibits. The very few designs that survive for these last spaces (and there are attractive capitals for which we have no designs) are marked by Waterhouse for the north corridor, or north galleries, but without specifying which wing or specific gallery.

The drawings arrived at the Museum bound into the two volumes. The first contained eighty-four sheets and the second fifty-two, with two larger format drawings on separate sheets. However, there is no clear distinction between the two volumes. They are now separately mounted and stored in archive boxes, which makes for easier study, although the original volume order is retained. As originally collected, the first four drawings show the Index Museum and Entrance Hall. Then follow ten designs for the south galleries on ground and first floors, and eleven for the external ornament of the gallery windows. Next come seventeen drawings for the principal entrance and Entrance Hall. Ten miscellaneous drawings are followed by a set of seven designs for the dormers of the façade. Ten more miscellaneous interior designs are succeeded by a set of designs for the large animals that decorate the parapet. Twenty designs for the south galleries are interspersed with a few exterior pieces and followed by designs for ventilation panels and for animals on the parapets of the pavilions and such things as the metal cresting of the main roof. The second volume closes with a series of seven panels for the principal staircase and fifteen for the boundary piers, with the lunette of the dodo making the final item. Evidently, the collection had only been cursorily assembled, and there does not appear to be a consistent logic behind the ordering. In my text, I have chosen to abandon the original ordering and present the drawings grouped according to the location for which they were designed. Chapter II, therefore, discusses the drawings in roughly the order a visitor might meet them.

Waterhouse clearly designed his creatures in groups, and the design sequence will have related loosely to the pattern of construction. I have already suggested that this may explain why the designs for the basement terracotta are missing – that the value of the drawings was not apparent until at least the lowest floor was up. In the light of what we know of the way in which the Waterhouse office worked, we may speculate further on the way these delicate drawings survived. For the whole of the period of construction there was a site office at South Kensington through which the designs will have passed. This is evident because so many of them are signed by the Clerk of Works. At the same time, and until almost the end of Waterhouse's career, the main office was at 61 New Cavendish Street.[6] The bulk of the working drawings will have been stored there, and, in theory at least, only copies of these were sent to South Kensington or the manufacturers. Copies of the sketches were, however, out of the question in an era before the photocopier. It would have been impossibly difficult to trace the concid freehand shading. Each sheet was unique and consequently precious. Presumably it was interest from the press that made the architect begin to realise the future worth of his drawings. Waterhouse was well aware of the value of publicity, and regularly sent drawings to the press for publication. His sketches will certainly have been requested alongside the more usual constructional drawings, plans and perspectives. Indeed, no less than ninety-seven of the creatures for which drawings survive (together with three for which they do not) were reproduced in *The Building News* during the period of construction.[7]

The next adventure for these small sheets of paper, following their storage in New Cavendish Street, was a move to Staple Inn Buildings in Holborn, a new office block added to the corner of the medieval Staple Inn when Waterhouse 'restored' it in 1887. In the early 1890s, the office moved into this new structure and remained there until World War II. Fortunately, since there was some bomb damage, the vast bulk of Waterhouse's architectural drawings had been transferred to a store in Reading around 1940, where they remained until donated to the RIBA in 1974. The assembly of this collection of sketches could have occurred on a number of occasions – when the museum building was completed, when the office moved to Staple Inn, or when Waterhouse retired a few years later. Given the occasionally random order, it seems unlikely that Waterhouse was himself responsible. He was, besides, remarkably modest about his buildings once they were completed, hardly ever setting out to advertise the potential heritage value of anything he built. It is much more likely that some member of the office staff (and I favour his faithful chief clerk J Willey) put the drawings together as an act of piety when 'the gov'nor', as he was affectionately known, retired.[8] It was probably at that point that they were taken from the office to the family home at Yattendon in Berkshire, which Paul Waterhouse inherited on his father's death. Since Michael, the grandson, lived nearby in Yattendon Grange, it is likely that he would have been able to rescue the collection once more when Paul died in 1924, retaining them until he began to prepare for his own retirement, and gave them to the Museum. Their miraculous escape from a series of those risks to which working drawings are subject is one more element in their importance. We may thank not only the artist and the donor, but also the anonymous compiler of the two volumes for their fortunate preservation.

The accompanying text, which also describes the processes of design and the means of manufacture, is supplemented with additional plates and descriptions of the sequence of painted and other decoration that enriches the terracotta of the interior. There is also a discussion of the potential sources for Waterhouse's designs, and his general ability as a draughtsman. In addition, I have cited a number of examples of terracotta in use on other buildings, both by Waterhouse and other architects, to show something of the tradition within which he was working. I have tried to present a rounded story that shows the context of the building, and that reveals the different parts taken by the principal players in achieving what is so utterly a building of its era. It is a story that has its share of controversy. Was the building modern or old-fashioned in its architecture? Who was responsible for what elements? And, finally, did it acknowledge the new Evolutionist science or merely display an outdated Creationism? Many parts of the story are obscure; and in some areas there is insufficient evidence to prove a case satisfactorily. However, I have taken the opportunity to speculate where I cannot produce absolute proof, in the hope that this extraordinary ornamental creation, this first Cathedral of Natural Science, can be seen as both the difficult compromise and the triumphant success that it was.

Notes

1 From the variations in size, and the traces of folding and stitching, it is clear that the sheets were pulled from two different sketchbooks. Two drawings are to a larger format. All the Sheets are reproduced here, with the exception of Volume II Sheet 14, which is blank and bears no marks of even having been used for preliminary study. The reason for its inclusion in the collection is obscure.

2 RIBA Drawings Collection, Drawings for The Natural History Museum (Wat 57 1–290). These are only a small number of those made. Figure 2 is numbered 13499/460F, indicating that it was a tracing (F) of the 460th drawing in the series for this building. There are also drawings indicating that a new series was begun for the many alterations made even before the building was opened.

3 Within the large Waterhouse Collection of the RIBA there are a number of cases in which one or two small drawings are tucked in among larger sheets, as in the furniture designs for Manchester Town Hall; but the sheer quantity of these pieces of paper will have made that method impracticable for The Natural History Museum.

4 Volume I is manually numbered, while a number stamp has been used for Volume II, suggesting either that they were assembled at different times, which seems unlikely, or that more than one hand was involved in collecting the sheets together.

5 The Museum (or its immediate surroundings) was struck by no less than eight bombs between 1940 and 1944. It is a tribute to the solidity of Waterhouse's construction that it was not seriously affected, though there was a certain amount of chipping and other damage to the decoration.

6 Originally number 8, then 20, and now 61, a blue plaque records this as the site of his office. It was also his home and subsequently that of his son, Paul, until the end of the century.

7 *The Building News*, Vol XXXV, 11 Oct 1878, facing p368; 25 Oct 1878, facing p422; 22 Nov 1878, facing p530; 29 Nov 1878, facing p558; 13 Dec 1878, facing p612; 20 Dec 1878, facing p640. The designs illustrated are not whole sheets, as reproduced here, but individual pieces such as single capitals, animals or roundels.

8 This nickname is preserved in the correspondence of the American architect, RS Peabody, who served briefly as a pupil in Waterhouse's office in 1869 and worked on Manchester Town Hall. (See RSP to MJDP, #115, 11 Aug 1869, SPNEA Collection, Boston, Mass, quoted in: Ann E. Robinson *The Resort Architecture of Peabody and Stearns in Newport, Rhode Island and Northeast Harbor, Maine* Tufts University MA Thesis 1999.) I am grateful to Ann E. Robinson for drawing this to my attention.

the drawings

Nature and Scope of the Drawings

The series of drawings that Alfred Waterhouse provided for the terracotta makers presents a remarkable combination of natural forms and ornamental patterns. The range is considerable, from the very low relief of the fishes (plate 100) or the greater depth of the flora in the various panels of the gallery piers (plate 108), to the fully three-dimensional modelling of the creatures that sit outside the windows of the first floor or crown the parapet. There is obviously a general sense of naturalism in the images of animals, especially in designs like that of the ibex in its roundel in the Entrance Hall (plate 81). No less than 106, out of a total of some 272 species are identified by their botanical or zoological names, even though these are more often generic than specific.[1] However, it is readily apparent that only some of the depictions are in any sense intended to be portraits. The 133 sheets,[2] many of which carry multiple images, include a number of abstract designs; and the conventional florets, so useful for filling the soffits of arches or for diapering walls, can hardly be considered as individual species. It is also difficult to be sure in some cases whether the foliage depicted is conventional or a conventionalised version of a specific plant. Even so, the identified proportion is high, when one remembers that most of the capitals and panels show at least two species – an animal and the foliage in which it rests – and that the many foliage capitals are carefully differentiated. In terms of artistic endeavour, observation and imagination, it is a considerable achievement. Its zoological and botanical value may be rather less. A modern scientist would probably cavil at the identifications given, or see only a passing resemblance to the species or genera named. But the whole point was to create ornament that would reflect the contents of the Museum, rather than precisely replicate the actual collections. Thus, the element of pattern that underlies each drawing is as crucial to its success as its naturalism, while the location of the various creatures on the building is sometimes as important as the depiction of the creatures themselves.

Surprisingly, the earliest dated design for these terracotta blocks does not belong to this series of fine pencil sketches. It is, instead, a drawing in black ink from the office archives showing details of the arches leading from the south galleries to the north corridor. The decoration consists of a band of twisted snakes and a variety of shell and plant patterns (fig 3).[3] These shell patterns are used again in the long corridor that links the Index Museum with the back galleries. However, no sketch survives of either the shells or the entwined snakes, and the draughtsmanship of the office drawing is by no means as attractive as the pencil sketches. Its relatively large scale[4] and the emphasis on outline deny it the delicacy of the pencil drawings reproduced here. It is tempting to believe that the office drawing is not entirely an autograph piece, though it is signed by Waterhouse, but was the work of one of his draughtsmen. However, that does not mean that Waterhouse will have been unhappy with its appearance.

3. A sheet of terracotta details signed and dated by Alfred Waterhouse (2 March 1874) represents some of the earliest designs for ornamental terracotta. The drawings are for the arches of the Entrance Hall, Index Museum and the arches leading into the south galleries. Although the ornamental creatures and plants are fairly crudely drawn, the sheet contains detailed instructions for fitting, and diagrams of the jointing of each block. (Sepia pen and sepia wash on tracing paper, 68.5 x 101.5 cm. Courtesy of the British Architectural Library, Drawings Collection)

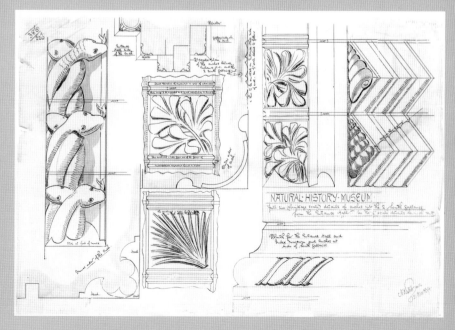

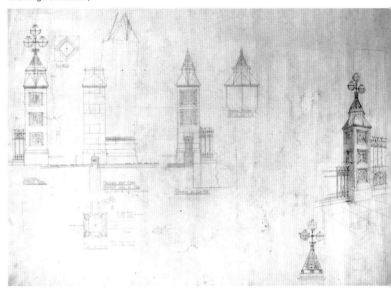

4. Different versions of the piers of the boundary fence. Sheet no 6614/343, showing the close attention Waterhouse paid to the appearance of his decoration, especially where it was close to the eye. (Pencil, 56 x 76.5 cm. Courtesy of the British Architectural Library, Drawings Collection)

12 Rather, it is likely that this is the sole survivor of what must have been a considerable number of intermediary drawings that bridge the gap between the sketches, with their feel for form, and the precise description of block sizes, which were needed for construction. Waterhouse himself presumably determined to control the details by producing small sketches and finding a modeller whom he could trust to turn them into three-dimensional models. The models in turn could then be used by the manufacturers to work from direct in casting the actual ornament. That decision to base the models on sketches and use more mechanical drawings to establish their setting is what led him to draw in pencil the remarkable menagerie that flutters and crawls or stares proudly out from the walls of almost every space in the Museum.

Whether the arrangement of the surviving sheets was the result of justification after the event or not, the first images in the volumes presented to the Museum may be taken to set the key. They show small birds in foliage on the jambs and voussoirs of the arches of the Index Museum (plates 1–2) and a series of agile monkeys climbing vertiginously up the soaring arches of the Entrance Hall (plates 3–4). The monkeys appear only in the one site, but the bird arches occur elsewhere in the museum – for instance, in the arches that link the west pavilions with the main galleries – and they thus have an important function in the overall unity of the design. They are also among the most charming of the images. Incorporating the varied and attractive poses of the birds perching in simple foliage with the straightforward mouldings of the basic terracotta blocks, Waterhouse manages to combine the lively depiction of the creatures with their careful disposition as architectural ornament.

The Gate Piers

This sense of ordered ornament is impressed on the viewer from the first moment of approach to the museum in the series of fifteen small, square panels for the Portland stone gate piers (plates 5–19). The finished terracotta for these pieces measures only 45 x 45 centimetres and they are among the most charming and intimate of the designs. Because they are set in panels in the gate piers, a number are encountered at eye level (fig 4); every visitor to the museum passes close by at least one set of these attractive pieces. The panels follow a similar compositional format. The animals chosen are all reproduced at something approaching actual size, and all are relatively small creatures since they have to fit on modest plaques. Among the most appealing are the brown sajou and the red squirrel (plates 7 & 16). Each animal is tightly bound into a spiral of foliage, and it is these that form the pattern of the blocks. Though the actual foliage is carefully distinguished and more or less identifiable, the stems are prominent in every case. So prominent in fact that in the case of the weasel (plate 6), the animal forms a decidedly minor element in the panel as a whole. The difficulty of making the smaller creatures fit identical panels is managed by providing some with more than one spiral, a creative decision that has the effect of adding variety without destroying the unity of the series. Thus, the tiny garden warblers (plate 19) flit through a plant with three spirals. Two black rats climb between four spirals (plate 14), as does the passenger pigeon – a little larger but solitary (plate 10) – which is one of the most popular of these designs. Sometimes, the animals' tails are pressed into the same service as the foliage. The spiral tail of the Senegal galago (plate 9) and the sajuo, for example, are vital parts of the composition, and, in the case of the pair of iguanas, it is the tails alone that provide the spirals.

Only the pair of formally intertwined asps (plate 11) and the cobra (plate 5), rearing up and spreading his hood, break this pattern. The cobra is particularly curious as a specimen of natural history, for it is named here as 'The Haje of Egypt', as though to create a deliberate link to the treasures of the Pharoahs, recently brought to the British Museum, thereby giving the old museum (from which The Natural History Museum was an off-shoot) and archaeology a shadowy presence in the new institution.

In all the panels, because the formal element of the pattern is so carefully confined to the background foliage, the overall impression is of naturalism in the creatures depicted and of considerable variety. The patterning afforded a degree of symmetry, against which could be set a diagonal movement by the creature depicted, thus enhancing the liveliness of the whole. The uniformity of scale on this series of plaques is important, not only because they are seen close up, but also because they are appreciated together. The visitor encounters all fifteen, three on each of the five piers, on approaching the gates, and the same fifteen in a different arrangement on the rear side. This is both an economical and creative way of introducing the idea of the museum and the scope of its exhibits on the visitor's first acquaintance with it. And yet the insistent repetition of spirals is important too in providing unity in what were, after all, only repeated indentations in a set of five identical gate piers. The (demolished) western gates presumably repeated the arrangement, though it is likely that the actual disposition of species was carefully altered to provide variety.

The Façade: Parapet and Skyline

Since it was essential that the ornamental menagerie should not take over and obscure the architecture, Waterhouse had the formidable task of designing a wide range of plants, fossils, birds and other animals that could be contained within the unity of his building. The consistent style of drawing and the faithful work of his modeller go a long way towards achieving the happy marriage of rich ornament and simple underlying form that make this building so memorable. It has to be remembered that even repeated patterns round a window required different models for each side, as well as for the voussoirs, keystone and stop-ends, each of which had to be specially drawn. It was not an easy task, and there were factors other than the designer's creativity to be considered.

The scale of the various creatures must have been a problem from the start. There is a careful intimacy in the way in which the small birds are handled in the arches of the Index Museum (plates 1 & 2), at precisely the height and scale they might have been seen in real life. At cornice level, by contrast, the animals, though fully modelled, regis-

ter largely as vertical accents on the long parapet. The panels of plants for the gallery piers have an obvious decorative quality, and, all drawn on sheets of roughly the same size, hardly mimic the growth patterns of the different species. It is typical of Waterhouse that each drawing shows the same close attention to eventual location and size as well as to form and texture, though each is executed to virtually the same dimensions. The similarity in size of the drawings tends to disguise the fact that Waterhouse was required to design for spaces, such as the gate panels, that would be seen close to, and others that would be seen from a distance of almost 150 feet.

Part of Waterhouse's success had always been his ability to create a romantic skyline for large buildings. The Natural History Museum was some 750 feet long and proportionately tall. Each wing consisted of eleven bays, stopped by a pavilion, and the roof-line of these immense blocks also had to be decorated with appropriately-sized figures. Here, Waterhouse designed four types, each of a slightly different scale (fig 5). On a Gothic building it was natural to provide gargoyles at cornice level. Then there were figures in roundels in the gabled dormer windows. Each dormer was intended to be capped by freestanding beasts, with further larger animals modelled in the round, on the parapet between them. At six foot in height, these are the largest decorative creatures of the whole scheme, and had to be made in two pieces.

5. A detail of a drawing of the roof-line clearly shows both the construction and the placing of the animals on the dormers. (Pen and coloured washes, whole sheet 56 x 76.5 cm. Courtesy of the British Architectural Library, Drawings Collection)

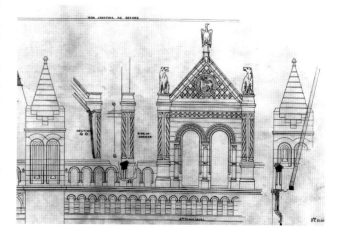

6. A dragon gargoyle adorns a corner of the London headquarters of the Prudential Assurance Corporation, which Waterhouse designed between 1896 and 1905.

14   Waterhouse provided only two designs for gargoyles for the south front (plates 22 & 23), which show him at his best in the sense that both versions are intensely decorative. They are, however, emphatically not portraits of any known species, even if carefully distinguished from each other. The way in which the manes are curled, like early Classical sculptures, are a reminder that his interests were those of a decorative designer and not of a scientist. He could indeed be quite flamboyant in his abstract designing and seldom lost an opportunity of 'enriching', as the Victorians called it, the various elements of the buildings he was constructing. Sometimes, he appears to have gone too far, for there is a note on one of his drawings for the Duke of Westminster's grand new house at Eaton: 'The Duke expressed a wish that / these [fire] dogs should not be repeated in any / other part of the Building, as he does not / like the lower part of them – His / Grace thinks that part too Assyrian in / Character.'[5] Gargoyles, however, were the stock-in-trade of any Gothic Revival designer. Waterhouse had already designed several and would produce a good many more, right up to the end of his career (fig 6).

   In contrast to the gargoyles, Waterhouse adopts a more determined naturalism in his designs for the dormer roundels (plates 24–30), though these are so far above the viewer that it is difficult to appreciate any naturalistic qualities. However, even here, Waterhouse allows the overall design to control the disposition of each animal. Seven designs survive – four of living species for the western galleries and three extinct ones for the east wing – and the groups are repeated along each wing. Of the seven designs, five represent four-footed beasts, each of which has its head turned neatly back to fit the circular frame. Only the pterodactyl and the eagle were not subjected to this treatment. In the case of the pterodactyl, there may have been a reason for this in the scientific sources (see p54), but the result is that two of the roundels have a contrasting composition that softens the insistent rhythm with the verticality of wings and body. There is considerable variation in the pencil-work in this group, which can only be explained by the assumption that Waterhouse had, by 1876 (more than halfway through the commission), established a sufficiently close working relationship with his modeller to be able to rely on him to extend the suggestions of each sketch appropriately. The palaeotherium, for instance, is marked by especially careful shading, which may be because Richard Owen had himself published on this particular beast.[6] The lively naturalism of the goat might be a reflection of Waterhouse's almost annual Alpine holidays. The dog, however, is less convincing and the eagle is more heraldic than naturalistic. The three creatures intended as finials, a pair of dogs or wolves at each side and an eagle at the apex, were dispensed with as an economy, but the designs appear a floor higher, on the parapets and gables of the pavilions (plates 31–33). The drawings for these were produced fairly late in the series.[7] Unusually, there are two views of the eagle, a front and side elevation, the latter of which appears particularly wooden, and it is almost a comfort to know that this view can only ever have been available to maintenance crews. They complete the menagerie of the parapet and are equally vigorously drawn, with heads fiercely raised, most baring their teeth, as though to ward off hostile visitors. They are not identified, merely named 'Animals in Pavilions', but they all have a distinctly wolfish appearance. Larger than the roundels, they are nevertheless not the largest creatures on the skyline.

   The real treasures of the parapet are the huge single beasts, a set of six designs, three living and three extinct, which are highly dramatic in their pencil work (plates 35–40). Fur, fangs and musculature are all boldly delineated and, appropriately for their lofty situation, several are drawn from a low viewpoint. The great palaeotherium appears again here, as another tribute to Owen, with a strikingly drawn head and boldly modelled forelegs. Oddly, for such important elements, there is only one drawing, and

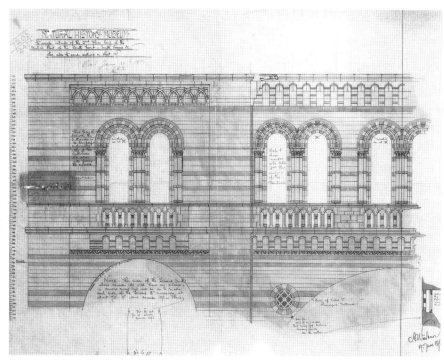

7. The drawing of half-inch scale details from the second floor level of the central part of the south front is dated 19 June 1876, a time when much of the ornamental work was being designed. The scale to the left of the image marks the individual courses of brick, which form the core of the wall, starting at 141 and ending at 273, which puts the main cornice at almost seventy feet above ground. (Sepia pen and sepia and green washes on tracing paper, 60 x 80 cm. Courtesy of the British Architectural Library, Drawings Collection)

no side elevations or even plans to show how they would fit on their bases. Presumably, the overall dimensions and the size of the base itself was sufficient for both architect and modeller. Instead, we are treated to four vigorous profiles, with only the lion and the mylodon drawn full frontal. These last two have boldly detailed coats, but the series as a whole offers a more even match between naturalism and pattern. The wolf for the western wing was drawn as early as August 1876, perhaps as a trial, and the others between January and May of 1877, shortly before they would have been needed. Set between the gables, four casts of each design are set up in an irregular rhythm to make a total of twelve beasts flanking the eleven gables. In the gables themselves, the four designs (the eagle appears on both wings) repeat in a regular pattern, forming a sort of counterpoint.[8] This interplay of two rhythms prevents an identical combination in any bay, and is an integral part of Waterhouse's decorative recipe, which should be considered alongside the designs for each individual creature.

Equally vigorous and more fiercely heraldic is the design (plate 41) for the gargoyle to the pavilion lunettes. Once again, vigorous pencil-work and dark shadow indicate the bold modelling that Waterhouse would require. These gargoyles are slightly smaller than those on the main cornice, and, though not much further away from the viewer, are made to look more distant by the way in which he drew only the fore parts of the lion-like creature he chose. This is yet another piece of evidence for the meticulous way in which Waterhouse imagined the prospective appearance of each piece in its eventual position. We find precisely the same attention to detail in the general construction. A note on one of the detail sheets for the second floor of the south façade, for instance, gives very precise instructions: 'The sides of the towers (south) above course 191 will have an entasis – a convex curve set out so as to make each side of the Towers 8" narrower at about 70' 0" above course 191' (fig 7).[9] Such a refinement would be all but invisible to the naked eye, though it would help make the towers appear taller and thus dramatise the building as a whole.

Another of the drawings (plate 42), which mixes an exterior detail with sketches for the plaster (carton pierre) ventilation roundels for the galleries, demonstrates this even more clearly, especially when compared with the construction drawings. There is precisely the same careful pencil work, clear outline and delicate shading. Figure 8 shows no less than three experimental versions of the same finial for the turrets of the pavilions. As we shall see later, the close collaboration between artist and sculptor appears to have led to the final choice. The same attention to detail can also be seen in the drawings (plates 43–47) of the simple rolled capitals for the windows in the south front, where the designs for the different levels (second and sixth floor windows are named) are carefully and subtly distinguished. Possibly the architect in Waterhouse was to the fore here, for the capitals shown in plate 43 seem more carefully drawn than the small, though attractive, bear's head for the Entrance Hall. Nor did Waterhouse confine himself to terracotta ornament. Plates 48 and 49 offer a set of delightful vignettes of creatures (the pterodactyl appears here for the third time on the building) designed to be made in cut metal for the cresting of the roof ridge. Their vigorous silhouettes bear a remarkable similarity to some medieval beasts he had sketched in Noyon a few years before, though there he was copying floor tiles (fig 9). Assembled into a continuous frame of foliate ironwork, these little creatures afford the final touch to the ornament of the exterior.

The crowning glory of the entrance bay, set high on the main gable, was a figure of Adam, as the highest of the primates and the peak of God's Creation. The figure is now lost, toppled, some say deliberately, at the end of World War II; and no drawings survive, so it is difficult to assess its quality. It is even unclear at what point the figure of Adam was chosen for this prime position. The earliest detailed design for the Museum[10] shows a flat parapet with two figures which one might expect would be Adam and Eve.

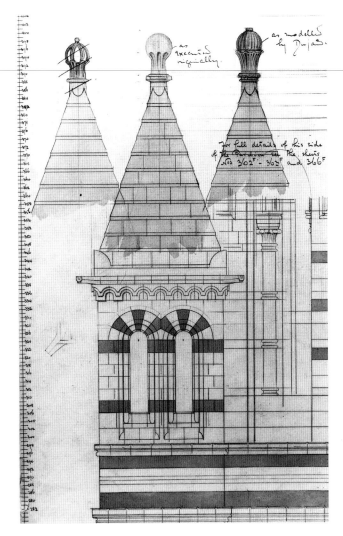

16

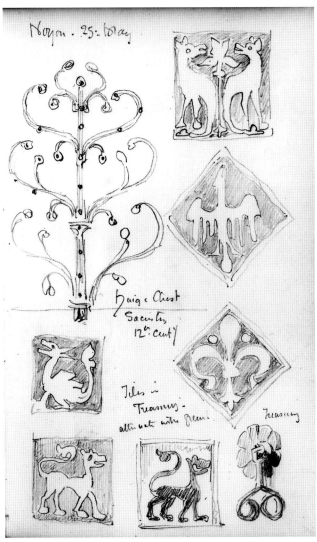

8. Left: Part of a sheet of working details of the Pavilions, showing alternative versions of the turrets at the angles. The three versions of the finials are interesting. One, 'as executed originally', was apparently superseded by that shown in plate 42 (Vol.II 15 of the drawings); but this is crossed out and apparently replaced by a third version modelled by Dujardin without a design by the architect. (Pencil and brown, green and pink washes, 76.5 x 56 cm. Courtesy of the British Architectural Library, Drawings Collection)

9. Below: Drawings of metalwork and tiles in the treasury at Noyon Cathedral of May 1869, barely a year after Waterhouse had produced his first designs for the museum, may be one of the sources for the distinctive animals of the roof cresting. (SB V, 10.5 x 16.5 cm. Private Collection)

However, since the same design shows a set of fourteen sculptured figures in niches around the main portal – a number which cannot be easily related to either Biblical or scientific symbolism – the whole iconographic identification of this early design must remain uncertain.

Equally uncertain is the quality, and even the authorship, of the figure itself. Early photographs (see fig.61) show only a distant figure reaching upwards. We do not know for certain that Dujardin had the necessary skill to work as a figure sculptor, a different class of work from modelling foliage and animals. And Waterhouse's own ability as a draughtsman in this area may also be in question. His skill in this line was in sketching small groups of people in costume and action that could be used to people his architectural perspectives. Only a single academic figure drawing (now lost) survived among his office archives;[11] but that was unsigned. It may very well be that he intended all along to commission another sculptor to make this figure, and that he did not draw a design himself. That would not have been unusual at the time. E.W.Godwin had done precisely that in 1860 when he specified figure sculpture for the façade of Northampton Town Hall, while admitting to friends that he had never done any life drawing. Godwin

teamed up with the sculptor Richard Boulton; and Waterhouse was in an equally good position to choose London sculptors such as Hamo Thornycroft. Although the designs and the sculptures are both lost, its position alone made it a key element in the iconographic scheme, and the choice of man, as the peak of the natural world, was probably inevitable. That the figure was thought of as Adam is equally unsurprising in the Christianist Creationist atmosphere of Richard Owen's circle in the 1870s.

The Façade: First-Floor Galleries

The main emphasis of the external decoration is centred on the first-floor galleries and the entrance. Each first-floor window, a Venetian form with two lights and circular tracery above, is enriched with one freestanding model of an animal and a pair of relief panels filling the space beneath the sill (fig 10). Here, one sees most clearly the distinction ordered by Owen between extinct species – which were to be displayed in, and were to ornament, the east wing – and living species, whose home was the west wing. Three fine sheets, each with a pair of designs, contain the two series of three that are repeated on west and east wings respectively (plates 50–52). Each animal sits on an outline of its base block and, to allow for the window, construction is cut off at the back where it fits tight against the wall. Waterhouse's sense of pattern comes through in the ingenious differences in the manes of five of these wonderful creatures, but they are all carefully shaded to show musculature. Four are drawn as though in elevation, but the Pterodactyl and what must surely be another extinct creature, although it has been tentatively identified as a Griffin,[12] are shown in perspective with their bases. Together, these figures make up some of the most clearly visible members of the decorative menagerie, for they are close enough to be seen clearly from the ground, and are modelled in the round.

Each is flanked by a pair of relief panels of fish, foliage or lizards (plates 53–56). Clearly, these creatures are best suited by their actual shape to fill long rectangular panels; fish and flowers, in particular, can be depicted well in relief. However, some of this series are a great deal more naturalistic than others. There are eight creatures in all, to the six freestanding ones, enabling Waterhouse to give every third pair of panels a different species, on each side of the window, while the other two are merely repeated casts of the same design. Interestingly, while the foliage is unidentified, the fish, here as in the interior, are all identified with their Latin names.[13] *Osteolepis* is drawn in what can only be described as a conventional fish pose, and its partner, *Dipterus macrotepidotus*, is even more naturalistic, shown as a carnivore evidently enjoying its prey, though the watery background is no more than hinted at. However, the pair of lizards for the east wing, *Amblyrhincus cristalus*, and the unnamed extinct plant, are drawn in improbably decorative poses. They certainly work as ornament, but constitute the sort of imagery that failed to impress the scientists at the time. The same is true of what appear to be hops for the

10. Base of a first-floor window in the east wing with the pterodactyl (see plate 51).

17

west wing, and the unidentified eel on the same sheet (on the building it partners the conger) is also unconvincing. The pair of designs on the final sheet of this series epitomises this contrast between decoration and naturalism. Although the conger is in effect neatly folded to fill its space, its head, fins, spiny crest and the shape of its tail are most carefully and convincingly drawn. The stomias on the other hand are drawn in a complicated but unrealistic pattern, similar to the extinct lizards of the east wing.

The final touch of ornament on the wings is found on the structural capitals to the window shafts (plates 57–60). A set of four drawings provides capitals for the mullions and for the windows of each wing. There are single capitals, alternating designs of plain foliage and beasts' heads in foliage for the central shaft and triple ones for the recessed orders of each side. There is something uncharacteristically hurried about the pair of drawings for the central mullions. It is not that they are less well-finished, but they are curiously unmatched. Those for the east wing have only a single wolf-like head, while three lions stare out from the design for the west wing. The lion is such a conventional ornamental creature that one wonders whether Waterhouse did not feel able to dash them off without having to think too much. Yet, as an ornamental capital, the lion version seems the more successful since it presents an identical face on each of the three matching sides. Both drawings are, however, oddly set out. The extinct wolf capital shows front and side view in perspective, but with the abacus of both sides drawn in elevation. Equally, the separate side view is drawn from below, as the capital would in fact be viewed, but with

11. An early drawing of the central part of the façade, dated 27 January 1872, bears an alternative version of one of the towers. The animal figures of the terracotta ornament of the main entrance have not yet been designed and only geometric patterns are shown. The drawing bears a Treasury stamp dated 14 July 1876, and the number 21 with the partly obscured initials suggests that this was part of the set of contract drawings. (Pen and coloured washes 78 x 50.5 cm. Courtesy of the British Architectural Library, Drawings Collection)

18

the whole upper section in elevation. The lion capital for the west wing is similar, except that its frontal view shows the upper part in proper perspective, with all its mouldings very carefully shaded. The triple foliage capitals for the two wings are also differentiated, each of the recessed columns having a slightly varied form. It is far from clear, however, whether these are intended to be different species, and the pattern of growth is entirely formalised. There was even a suggestion in one of the architect's drawings, published during the construction period,[14] that a lion's head might be used as a further alternative for the innermost of the recessed shafts.

The Principal Entrance

The highlights of the façade, the central towers and main doorway (fig 11), have been much illustrated and discussed. It is a tremendous composition, its towers, like the *westwerk* of a Cathedral, flanking the two-storey entrance. The portal itself – one can hardly call it a doorway – is set within no less than eight recessed columns, which themselves enclose minor colonnettes (fig 12). It is no surprise, therefore, to find that a total of sixteen drawings concentrate on this area alone (plates 61–76). The sketches were mostly produced in the late summer and autumn of 1875, and the final design, by then completed, was illustrated in *The Building News* in December 1878.[15] The famous watercolour elevation of the doorway[16] shows a simplified earlier decorative scheme, with fewer animals and merely a foliage frieze above the doorways. By the time the terracotta blocks were being designed, Waterhouse had found ways to enrich this somewhat. Given the constant battles for funding with the Treasury, this was clearly something of an achievement.

The bases of the shafts are decorated with tiny heads or foliage, almost lost in the overall richness (plate 61). Unfortunately, no separate drawings survive for the varied ornamentation of the recessed shafts themselves, but their patterns are visible beneath their capitals in plate 65. Waterhouse offered no less than six designs for bands, or annulets, round the middle of each shaft. Since the series is labelled D to I, it seems likely that he produced a further three versions. If so, they were rejected as unsuitable, as was design H, for the doorway is enriched with only five different annulets. Three of the chosen designs, D, F and I, are variations of conventional foliage twists, but two, E and G, have mice or frogs among the leaves. It is typical of Waterhouse to indulge in a number of variations of orna-

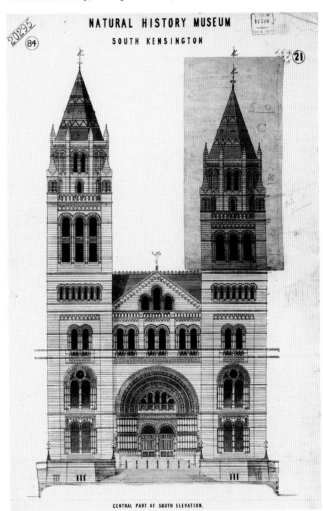

NATURAL HISTORY MUSEUM
SOUTH KENSINGTON

CENTRAL PART OF SOUTH ELEVATION.

ment in this way. His ingenious mind was always ready to devise yet another way of turning a tendril or folding a leaf. We are left to wonder whether pieces of ornament – animal, mineral or vegetable – were designed in alternative versions, and how many were rejected and destroyed. This appears to be almost the only case in which an unused alternative survives.

The architectural glory of the entrance itself is the set of a dozen brilliantly delineated capitals for the major and minor orders of the archway. These may be compared to the delicate plant portrayals that were still being carved for the Oxford University Museum. Yet here, while all are care-

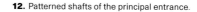

tion above. The great tympanum of the arch is filled with a 19
five-light window, divided by shafts, whose designs are
included on the sheets. But the principal interest in the
ornament is the set of five panels below the windows filled
with portraits of mammals, all carefully named (plates
70–74). To one side are a jaguar and a kangaroo, while the
American brown bear and the hyena fill the two panels on
the other. The central panel displays a lioness encircled by
a particularly fierce, large-headed snake. The final touch
is the pair of heads peering from the spandrels above
(plate 75). The five panels and the spandrels are another
example of Waterhouse's naturalistic portrayal of species.
Significantly these, too, are identified like the animals on
the parapet and several of the window panels. However, the
identification is not consistent in a scientific way. The monkey is identified as no more than 'monkey' and the central
panel, with its improbable struggle, bears no identification.
The double figure makes an important accent in the centre
of the doorway, but it is almost as though Waterhouse was
less interested in the species in this instance. A sense of pattern is to the fore at this point, something that underlies
the naturalistic portrayal all over the great portal.

The Entrance Hall

The subtle mixture of pattern and portraiture continues as
soon as the visitor enters. The rear face of the central shaft
of the doorway is treated to the same forest of formalised
foliage, this time inhabited by a pair of parakeets, a fox and
a wild cat (plate 76). Passing through, the visitor stands in a
dark, vaulted hall that opens into the Index Museum. For
this space, Waterhouse designed a set of four creatures for
the springing of the vaults (plate 77). They are among the
most delightful of the designs he created and are deservedly
picked out by feature lighting. The four creatures are all
shown in a foliage setting on one sheet, and are repeated in
each compartment of the vault. The leafage is carefully differentiated on the drawing, as so often in this collection,
and the animals named. The iguana can be compared to
that on the gate piers (plate 8), but here, it is more boldly
modelled for a larger scale, and, in any case, the precise
species is not given. Yet all this is scarcely noticed by the visitor, standing beneath the dark vault of the first floor with
the light and height of the Index Hall leading forward.

Waterhouse distinguished between what he called the
Index Hall and the Entrance Hall, treating the first three
bays of the building, to the back wall of the main east and

fully distinguished, none is identified as a portrait of a particular species. The basic form of the capital clearly
required a degree of formalisation in the patterns of
growth, and it is quite possible that Waterhouse felt freer to
depart from naturalism here in the interests of his
Romanesque Gothic style. The capitals he drew, however,
are among the most striking of the whole series, deeply
shaded and crisply drawn. Waterhouse labelled them A to L
in a series that will have allowed the builder to identify the
precise placing of each different block, and the pattern of
repeats that Waterhouse intended. The upper capitals of
each side, for instance, have a pattern of repeats, D, B, C, B,
C, B, C, A, and E, G, F, G, F, G, F, H, across the recessed
orders on left and right respectively. Nor was this all, for the
double doorway itself was provided with especially rich capitals, level with the annulets of the columns, in which a variety of small birds and a mouse, together with a wader, a dog,
a stork and what looks very like a baboon, sit or stand in further patterns of plants.

Above all this, the arch itself was further enriched. At the
level of the main capitals, Waterhouse designed a frieze in
which at least six different creatures are fitted into the formal spiral of the foliage (plate 69). This is altogether
lighter and more delicate than his first design, allowing a
much greater prominence for the main naturalistic decora-

20

C. H. Dixon, Photo.

west galleries, as the entrance (fig 13). This is the space occupied by the dramatic flying stair from first to second-floor; Waterhouse's concept allowed for a pause on entering, with the Index Museum framed by the arch of the stair. The spaces flow together, but the terracotta ornament was separately considered. Only the painted ceilings of the gallery continue an identical recipe through both spaces. Ground-floor capitals for the Entrance Hall were drawn in 1875. A year later, Waterhouse was at work for the same space, designing a pair of ventilating panels for the second-floor ceiling (plate 78). Presumably, the terracotta panels for the grilles at first-floor level (plate 79) were already fitted. They seem to have slipped through Waterhouse's system without name, date or signature; but they are there to this day. Although these might be considered minor elements in the decoration, all three are, nonetheless, fine designs of a conventional form, drawn with loving attention to detail. The shaping of the spiral stem for the left-hand panel, used for the living species on the west, is particularly carefully handled.

Only after passing through the Index Museum, up the grand stairs and back to the front of the building, does one find the final elements of Waterhouse's conception for the ornament of the Entrance Hall. Set in roundels (plates 80 & 81), these are carefully studied pieces, delicately shaded and detailed, the legs of the two herons and an ibex, along with other elements, flowing outside the main circle to give a greater immediacy to the modelled figures. These two roundels are some of the best of Waterhouse's animal portraiture and, though judiciously posed, have a real sense of portraying living creatures. Waterhouse repeated the

recipe at the approach to the Refreshment Room at the other end of each gallery. Contemporary photographs show how these fine pieces, in their circular frames, are well adapted to the space for which they were designed (fig 14). The continuity of space may have been in Waterhouse's mind when he drew the various designs for the balustrade of the Index Museum galleries on the same sheet as one of the triple capitals for the entry (plate 68). The final sketch for the Entrance Hall (plate 82) makes the same point, in that its four designs for the shafts that support the topmost floor, where the Index Museum galleries run round beneath the flying stair, are clearly labelled for the Entrance Hall; yet one is also marked 'For side Galleries First Floor Index Museum'.

The Index Museum (Central Hall)

The Index Museum, together with its great stairway, is undoubtedly the architectural climax of the whole building. Both the drawings and the decoration itself demon-

15. The rich cornice and balustrade at the springing of the iron arches of the Index Museum. The triangular braces of the arch are filled with a range of foliage patterns.

strate how determined Waterhouse was to bring off an architectural coup in this memorable space. Here, he used more than just the terracotta for which we have drawings. Stained glass, decorative ironwork and, above all, paint, are deployed to stunning effect. The painted decoration, here and in the smaller hall designed as a Museum of British Natural History, amply complement the modelled animals and demonstrate once again Waterhouse's skill as a designer. The Entrance Hall is distinguished by its soaring arches of terracotta with their tribe of acrobatic monkeys (plates 3 & 4). The light, airy quality of the whole space is thus secured, and there is a distinct transition from the covering to the walls, which sport so much moulded ornament (fig 15). The main roof is spanned by light iron arches, themselves set with patterns of foliage in gilt metal, and over both spaces hover the painted panels of the ceiling.

To accompany this splendour of plant portraits, Waterhouse used animal depictions sparingly in the terracotta ornament of the Index Museum itself. A mere four sheets, in addition to the bird and monkey arches, contain the designs for the Index Museum (plates 1–4, 83–86). One of these is more than half-filled with a simple foliate pattern for the soffits of the monkey arches; another jostles together balustrade shafts and rosettes for the interior with rosettes[17] and column bases for the principal entrance. Two of the sheets have details of blocks for archways, lightly ornamented with sprigs of laurel. There are eight different blocks, together with two plain moulded ones, used in the double arches of the Entrance Hall gallery, not the Index Museum itself. Their simpler pattern acts as a contrast to the greater richness of the bird arches of the ground floor and the bold shapes of the monkey arches. It is yet another example of Waterhouse's care in the disposition of ornament. And the same care can be seen in the capitals of the Index Museum piers, which are in the form of animals in formalised foliage (plate 86). They are similar to those above the principal entrance, but slightly less delicate, which is appropriate since they would be seen from a long way below. Then there are two more versions of the capitals for the side galleries, and one for the arcade between the Index Museum and the Refreshment Room. This leaves only a series of six animal-head corbels, which are repeated in each bay of the Index Museum. They are delicately drawn and carefully individualised, but they are scarcely portraits; indeed, the bulldog verges almost on caricature. What makes them particularly interesting, however, is the

difference between the sketch (plate 84) and the block fitted in the building (fig 15). They are drawn as though facing ahead on the level; but they are modelled to stare down at an angle into the hall. Clearly, Waterhouse was able, by this stage, to rely on his modeller to interpret the information on sketches in a way that was appropriate for the ornament's eventual setting. Sadly, these beasts are virtually invisible high up under the roof springing (see fig 15). It is one of very few mistakes in the disposition of the ornament, and is a pity, for they are attractively sketched. For the most part, however, Waterhouse used only repetitions of simple shaped blocks and patterns of blue and cream terracotta in this space (fig 16). In the same way, he restricted himself to formalised ornament in the designs for rosettes and balustrades of the principal staircase and first-floor galleries (plates 68 & 87).

The repetition of simplified forms on the staircase is used to set off the series of fourteen naturalistic portrayals in panels set in the piers of the great stair (plates 88–94). Here, as in the roundels or the gate piers, Waterhouse had only to control the poses of his creatures so that they fitted their panels, but there is less emphasis on pattern. All but one of the species are carefully identified, usually with both Latin and common name, and there is a clear differentiation of the foliage to suggest varied habitats. Like those on

22

16. Detail of a drawing of the second-floor galleries of the Entrance Hall, signed and dated 7 July 1876, demonstrates the richness and complexity that Waterhouse achieved by repetition of a limited number of ornamental elements. On either side of the arch are the spaces for the monkey arches. (Sepia pen and green and sepia washes on tracing paper, whole sheet 39.5 x 78.5 cm. Courtesy of the British Architectural Library, Drawings Collection)

the panels of the gate piers, these creatures can be seen close to and, since the stair was not used for exhibits, they were presumably more easily examined than most of the modelled ornament. Here again, Waterhouse restricts himself to the smaller mammals and birds, so that, though the panels measure no more than 36 x 58 centimetres, the creatures can be portrayed life-size. They are naturalistically portrayed (with a realistic mix of single creatures, pairs or adults with young), if not scientifically accurate, though it should be acknowledged that modelled clay is not the best medium for imitating fur and feathers. The black grouse, which the Victorian gentry (following their Queen to Balmoral and the Highlands) were busy shooting and eating, is shown with a brood of four chicks.

One final element remained to be decorated. The north wall of the Hall is broken by the windows of what was designed as the Refreshment Room (fig 17). These are filled with stained glass, which Waterhouse designed as patterns of conventional leaves and rosettes. Neither form nor colour are used for anything approaching scientific description, though that would certainly have been possible. Instead, Waterhouse used the pale tints and muted colours that are typical of his glass elsewhere. The windows thus fit well with the painted ceiling, adding a jewel-like quality to the high wall when seen lit from behind. Above them, taller windows are left plain to light the hall. The wall itself, however, still needed to be treated to some decoration, if only to break up its bulk (plates 95–97). Here, Waterhouse reverted to his compromise of naturalistic por-

trayals in formalised foliage, matching the entrance with a series of enriched shafts, arcading, and a further series of animal capitals for the blind arcade that separates the two tiers of windows. The capitals in particular are a fine set, drawn to a larger format, as though they were considered special. Certainly, they are as varied and elaborate as those on the principal entrance, though, like the capitals of the main piers, they are almost too distant to see. As a final touch, Waterhouse provided tiny gablet pieces on which perch a series of four spirited creatures.

The Refreshment Room lobbies (Central Hall and Plant Power Exhibition)

In Waterhouse's plan, the Index Museum was backed by a first-floor Refreshment Room with a Museum of British Natural History beyond it. The decoration of the room itself did not involve much moulded terracotta. Two versions of formalised rosettes are set in the spandrels of the windows, which have sills of polished stone. The impression is that this space was deliberately left freer than the rest of the Museum, which would be in keeping with its function as a Refreshment Room, the sort of space for which Waterhouse generally preferred to use glazed tiles for sanitary reasons. However, the lobbies to the Refreshment Room were considered separately, and their principal decoration consists of delicately stencilled ceilings. These spaces are approached through archways from the Index Museum gallery, which bear roundels of terracotta, effectively completing the ornament of the main body of the Museum, though Waterhouse labelled them as belonging to the Refreshment Room. They depict South American fauna in the shape of a rhea and a mazama (plates 98 & 99) and are comparable to the very best of Waterhouse's other designs, delicately shaded and drawn with great attention to the textures of feathers and gently

23

swelling musculature. The finished panels face down the long galleries of the Index Hall to the goat and herons in the Entrance Hall. Finally, beyond the Refreshment Room, the Museum of British Natural History, now the Waterhouse Café, was less richly-modelled than the Index Museum. No separate designs survive for this space, whose decoration uses many of the standard ornamental blocks employed elsewhere in the Museum. Yet the space, which is a smaller version of the Index Museum, derives its own quality from its painted ceiling.

The East and West Galleries

If Waterhouse was not able to indulge to the full his love of terracotta in the Refreshment Room, there were still major spaces to be enriched in the shape of the display galleries at the front of the building. These were arranged on three floors, though the terracotta ornament was concentrated on the ground and first floors, where the frame structure of the museum required iron uprights to be clad in some decorative material. Here, terracotta had another use: as a fire-proof covering. For each gallery, therefore, Waterhouse provided not only decoration for the wall surfaces and window openings, but cladding for the two rows of twenty piers that ran down the centre, together with matching pilasters at each end. These galleries would provide a great opportunity to demonstrate the principals on which Owen had organised the Museum. The east wing was to be devoted to extinct species, and the west to living. It was a division that was to prove something of a millstone, for it tied the museum to a narrowly creationist approach, rather than to the modern evolutionary view of natural history. For Waterhouse, however, one suspects that it merely offered another chance to display his ingenuity and virtuosity as a designer. No less than thirty sheets of designs survive for these galleries and their pavilions (plates 100–129).

For the galleries, Waterhouse designed three tiers of decoration. The letter sequences he gave to the two types of ornament for which most sketches survive make no distinction between east and west wings. This suggests that he was thinking in terms of whole sets of capitals and foliage panels, rather than contrasting decoration for the 'extinct' and 'living' galleries, evidently seeing the designs as a single ornamental sequence. The groups of closely-matched, precisely-balanced designs are therefore presented and discussed together. The base of each pier and pilaster was covered with low-relief panels of fishes, while the upper

piers were divided into two, set with panels of flora in higher relief. Finally, each one was crowned with a pair of fully-modelled capitals. Following Owen's division, Waterhouse used the same sets of species for ground and first floors in each wing, but avoided monotony by a different arrangement of the piers (figs 18 & 19). The lower first-floor galleries, originally intended to accommodate twelve-foot display cases – a foot taller than those on the ground floor – have a single foliage panel in place of the three on the lower floor.

The designs for the east wing, which head the series, were not the first to be sent for manufacture. Those for the east ground floor are dated April 1875, and for the first floor from June 1878. Work clearly began on the west wing, where a trial capital is dated May 1874; the ground-floor panels were sent for casting in December 1874, with the first floor following in September, October and November 1877. Only a single set of fish designs for the pier bases survives; and that is undated. Twenty-four carefully-labelled extinct species are laid out on two sheets (plates 100 & 101) for the east galleries. Presumably those for the living galleries are lost. Each fish is tightly-drawn in profile, set at an angle on its block. Four designs have the water lightly marked in, and this was incorporated in all the blocks, giving a consistent texture to the lower section of each pier. One has the distinct impression that the fish were directly copied from a book, for they are drawn in simple profile with no attempt to show turning or movement, which was precisely the convention adopted for scientific book illustrations of fish (fig 20). In Waterhouse's sketches, there is also more precision than in many of his other drawings. They were, however, designed for the lowest relief, and would only be partly seen behind or between display cases. Possibly they held less interest for their designer as a result, though they may be among the more scientifically accurate of his designs.

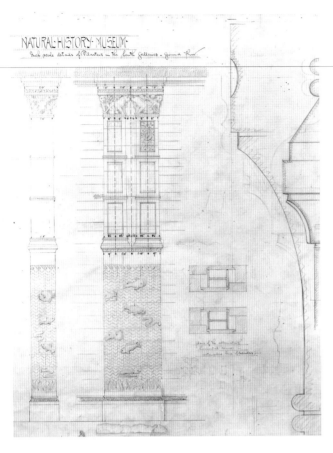

18. Elevations of the pilasters in the ground-floor galleries of the south front show how the various ornamental parts fit into a single composition. Here the ornamental detail is merely sketched in; but there are detailed plans to show how the terra-cotta blocks are jointed and fitted round the steel structure. (Pencil, 63 x 56 cm. Courtesy of the British Architectural Library, Drawings Collection)

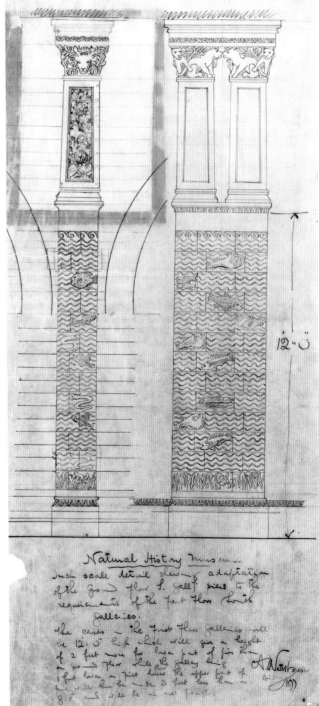

19. Elevation of the south gallery piers to show how the design for the ground floor is adapted for the different height of the first floor. This drawing dates from 4 May 1877, when much of the ornament was already designed and had been sent to the manufacturers. (Sepia pen on tracing paper, 72 x 32 cm. Courtesy of the British Architectural Library, Drawings Collection)

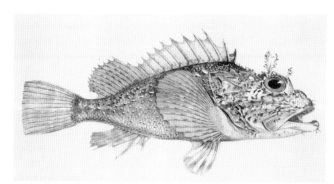

20. *Scorpaena histio* natural size (31 x 24 cm) from: *Zoology of the Voyage of HMS Beagle under the command of Captain Fitzroy, R.N., during the years 1832–1836* Smith Elder, London, Vol. III, Part IV, Fish, 1847, pl. 8

East and West Galleries: Plant Panels

There is both more life and more variety in the plant panels and capitals, of which designs for both east and west galleries survive. The series of foliage designs are among the most attractive, combining a degree of accurate depiction with Waterhouse's usual strong sense of pattern, a disciplined approach that was essential if they were to fit the narrow panels on the piers. For the east galleries, six different designs, labelled G to L, survive for each of the ground and first floors (plates 102–106). The smaller panels for the ground floor are carefully, though not strongly, differentiated, but with the taller panels for the first floor, Waterhouse managed to make more of a decorative statement. He places more emphasis on the stems, in two cases adding a repeating diamond pattern that threads in and out of the leaves (plates 104–106). The decorative designer in him comes out strongly here, as does the architect with a feel for siting, in the way he emphasises the vertical perspective by diminishing the leaves on the plants. The describer of natural history is there too, as evidenced in the fact that four of the plants are identified, though the remaining two are merely listed as 'Extincts'. For the west ground floor, six variations of the pomegranate are labelled A and A* to C and C*, with a further three designs of *Anona paulustris* as D, E and F making nine in all (plates 107–109). These alternate with the pomegranate panels in sets of eighteen for each pier, giving a slightly richer cast to the west galleries.[18] For the living plants on the first floor, Waterhouse's designs are all built round intertwining spiral stems, which give a curvilinear pattern in contrast to the rather stiff stems and diamond patterns of the fossilised plants (plates 110–112). However, the extra richness of this wing is continued here, for three of these plants stems are inhabited – by a chameleon, a lerot and some parrots. There is more variety, too, in the drawing of the leaves, as though the artist were intent on making them appear more alive than their counterparts in the east wing. Yet, although the foliage is carefully distinguished, only three of this series are identified, while the inclusion of the various creatures gives the impression that Waterhouse is closer to drawing anonymous decorative foliage in the manner he had used so effectively in the frieze above the entrance.

East and West Galleries: Capitals and Relief Panels

The concept of a single design series for both east and west galleries is even clearer with the capitals, which are labelled A to X. G is drawn with the first plant panels (plate 107) and appears to have been a trial piece. It is more frequently used than the other capitals, and presumably replaces H, which is missing and seems to have been an alternative design that was never used. One design, two versions of coralline foliage (X), is not assigned to a specific wing, though it is used in the east. This reinforces the idea that Waterhouse himself was less concerned to draw distinctions in the decoration than to give consistency to the sets of main display galleries, but in devising so many variations it appears that he found a good deal of scope for imagination and ingenuity. The basic recipe is simple: plain foliage alternates with beasts' heads appearing out of a leafy background. The drawings are finely handled, but there is a slightly caricatured quality to some of the beasts, and they are generally not the most convincing of his depictions. This may be simply because Waterhouse's skill was not that of an animal or figure painter; but it is also partly a matter of scale. The 'horse's' head of capital A, for instance, is either an improbably small attempt at Eohippus, or peers out from a patch of unnaturally large grasses. There are also occasional disparities of scale between the two animals of a pair of capitals. The dog design of J for the west gallery, for example, is awkwardly scaled with its neighbour, which might be a Shetland pony.

Set high up against the ceiling beams, these capitals are not as clearly seen as the panels on the staircase; it may be that Waterhouse was more concerned with their practical and visual function as capitals than with the actual imagery. Since the upper piers were treated as square and set in pairs, there were effectively six visible faces to design for

26 each stanchion. The six designs A–F and I–N are reserved for the side pilasters of the galleries, with P and Q additionally for the pilasters of the west ground floor. The main piers and responds at each end are decorated with repeats of four designs each, U–X in the east galleries and G and R–T in the west. Two pairs for each wing have identified species, while two are anonymous. For increased richness, Waterhouse designed them, with the exception of G, as pairs, of which each half is different. Yet the simple band of chevron ornament on the abacus and the consistent concave curve of the foliage do much to bring unity to this menagerie. The foliage on all the capitals is carefully differentiated, though none of the plants are identified, and some cannot be readily recognised as accurate depictions of any particular species. The west wing has more flowing or fruiting plants than the east, perhaps to stress their living quality, but the pattern of growth of some of them – K, for instance – is, to say the least, improbable. It seems that Waterhouse is, as usual, compromising between natural depiction and pattern, with a certain preference for the latter. This can be clearly seen in the two owl capitals (plate 122), where the birds spread their wings in a usefully symmetrical way as they fly out of some foliage that is a cross between oak leaves and seaweed. The two cat capitals (plate 120) further support this thesis. The cats are provided with patterned manes, which are less naturalistic than decorative, more in keeping with the formalised capitals of the entry than the rest of this series. They are also the only capitals on which a whole creature is drawn; the cats are depicted as though involved in action, stalking through the foliage. In what seems to be almost the only touch of humour in this rich but rather serious ensemble, one stares down towards the fish at the base of its pier. Finally, within this carefully consistent series there is one variant for each wing. In most cases, the relief projection of the side faces is only sketched in, if it is shown at all. However, on one design for each wing, sheets V and S, Waterhouse drew out the side faces fully, with an additional species in profile, and in both cases the species are all named. In the west wing, the wolf and brown bear are joined by the boar; and, in the east wing, *Anoplotherium vulgaris* and *Xiphodon gracile* keep company with Owen's dinosaur, the palaeotherium. The decoration of each gallery is completed by a relief tympanum over the doorway to the private stairways. The east wing has an image of the dodo (plate 127), and the west a similar panel with monkeys; only the dodo design survives.

It is among the most elaborate of the drawings, in which delicate pencil-work is combined with the sort of clear definition that was essential for the modeller. The image is deservedly well known, even if current research suggests that the recently extinct dodo may have been scrawnier than depicted here.[19]

East and West Pavilions

Beyond each gallery, Waterhouse had arranged a smaller space in the pavilions that formed the terminations of his long façade. These, too, had their own decoration, though less rich and varied than the galleries. The designs for this are preserved on three sheets, with those for east and west wings both on the same sheet (plates 128–130). Waterhouse devised two more plant panels and a further pair of foliage capitals for the pilasters. They follow closely the general recipe for the galleries, though the plant panels, particularly that for the east gallery, have more strongly-marked trellis patterns threading through the foliage. Each pavilion is approached through a wide archway, which is decorated with birds in foliage. Sadly, separate designs for these do not survive, and alterations have now concealed much of the terracotta. The west pavilions appear to repeat the bird arches of the Index Museum, but those in the east wing have different species, among which the pterodactyl appears once more.[20] However, the first of the surviving sketches for the pavilions allows us to consider further elements of the interior, for it also contains drawings for a set of twelve small corbels for other areas of the museum. In addition to the main façade, the Entrance Hall, Index Museum and other principal spaces that we have examined, there were still extensive study galleries to the rear that were faced in terracotta and decorated. For these spaces too, Waterhouse needed to provide designs and to arrange a layout of decorative elements.

The North Corridor (Waterhouse Way) and North Galleries

The most interesting decoration in the north corridor, is in the form of capitals with owls and monkeys; unfortunately, the designs for these do not survive. However, the progression from south galleries or Index Museum to the corridor and back galleries follows a typically Victorian hierarchy of diminishing richness. Yet each archway and cornice has its own share of decoration. The building required a host of minor decorative details from corbel stones to enrichment bands and it is clear that Waterhouse was ready to devise patterns even for the least of these. For the most part, the smaller details are sketched in the margins of the various major items, as for instance in plate 1. There are a number of sheets of mixed details, which I have already discussed with reference to their principal image. Plates 131 and 132, however, demonstrate clearly what Waterhouse was doing. One shows a set of foliage corbels for the north east, or back, galleries, dated January 1875, with a base, dated to April of the same year for shafts at the north end of the north galleries. The dates and locations reflect the progress of the different parts of the structure. Thus the same date saw Waterhouse sketching an ornamental base for the lamp post at the principal entrance, the sort of detail most likely to be added after the main structure was up. It also shows a revision of this detail dated to June 1875. The second sheet has details of a laurel band, with leaves meeting at the keystone, which is used for archways in a number of locations. Set beside this are two rosettes for archways on the south side of the Entrance Hall: four animal-head corbels for the exterior of the third floor of the towers and even a simple capital for balustrades to the balconies in the second floor of the towers and the gallery between them. Such details are scarcely noticed by the visitor, yet it is typical of Waterhouse that he gave his attention equally to minutiae of this sort as to the overall structure and composition; his ability to do this is what underlies the consistency and quality of the building as a whole. Waterhouse carried his inventive designing through to the last detail (though it is worth noting that the roundels of the basement windows reappear in what were originally the narrow study galleries). The Collection includes two sheets with five different designs for plaster panels for the back galleries (plates 133 & 134). Each design is worked out both as a running ornament in long panels and as a square unit for turning corners. These panels may not be as rich as those designed for the Entrance Hall (plate 79), but they are just as ingeniously varied. Neither sheet is finished, but the drawings give enough information for the modeller to create what were, after all, units for repetition. Alterations and the insertion of false ceilings make it difficult to see the panels; but one version can be clearly seen in what is now the bookshop.

The Porters' Lodges

The final touch, since it was the last element to be constructed, was the pair of small lodges by the gates for the porter, of which only one survives.[21] This little building, with its tall pyramidal roof and chimney, is treated to exactly the same sort of decoration as the Museum itself (plates 47 & 135). It did not rate the same degree of ornamentation as the main building, however, being low down in the hierarchy of the whole. Yet the design of the little cornice blocks is as finely finished as any of the other drawings. Perhaps the most attractive touch is the large lion's head in its roundel. It is set in the rear wall of the Lodge, and thus unseen to the visitor entering the Museum. You pass it as you leave, and in many ways it typifies the Waterhousian recipe for the ornament. The design is scrupulously drawn, with delicate shading for the musculature of the beast's face, but the creature, though recognisably a lion, is treated to a beautifully-curled mane that effectively removes it from any sense of natural depiction. In its billeted circular frame, it breaks the monotony of the rear wall and links the unique terracotta of the Museum itself with the more commonplace heraldic lions of the gateway (fig 21).

Throughout this remarkable series of designs, there is a delight in precise pencil-work that leaves no doubt as to the final form, but which is aesthetically pleasing in its own right. The way in which Waterhouse laid out so many of the sheets suggests that he too saw them as such. It is perhaps significant that all the most important decorative pieces are treated to individual sheets, or drawn in pairs, like the gallery capitals. Only with the lesser ornament does Waterhouse jumble corbels from one area with rosettes for another. Incomplete as it is, the collection is still a *tour de force*. The very survival of so many, from what must undoubtedly have been a larger series,[22] is a piece of extraordinary good luck. One has to remember what a chequered history the individual sheets will have had, drawn by Waterhouse, checked by the Clerk of Works, passed to the sculptor who made the models and then perhaps sent down to the factory before being returned to the architect. There they would have joined the hundreds of other working drawings that filled the drawers of Waterhouse's office in New Cavendish Street, or sent over to the printers of *The Building News* for engraving. Fortunately for us, they were mostly returned, and the office was organised efficiently enough for the bulk of them to be kept. We may speculate

that the aging Waterhouse occasionally leafed through them with pleasure in the years after his building was completed.

This study of the drawings has shown how Waterhouse steered a compromise between pure decoration and naturalistic depiction. If he was not always totally successful in this, he nonetheless created a number of memorable pieces and an ensemble that is an unforgettable architectural experience. It remains to set the drawings, and other decorative designs, in context. There is more to this design effort than a sequence of superb pencil sketches or a range of unusual terracotta sculptures. The disposition and meaning of the sculptures can be endlessly debated, but the decorative scheme that stems from these fine sketches is the end result of a series of different creative efforts. Waterhouse was the artist, and his skill speaks for itself. He was also the architect who saw the scheme to fruition, and managed to avoid his building being impoverished by government parsimony. Yet he was not the originator of the scheme, and the opinions of his client, Richard Owen, were equally important. Finally, of course, the concept of the naturalist and the sketches of the architect had to be turned into a three-dimensional reality. The drawings are not only a testament to the designer's skill, but also the starting point for the development of the scheme as a whole.

21. An iron gate pier is topped by a finely-modelled gilded iron lion.

30

Notes

1 The appendix on p188 lists the species identified with their locations in the buildings and their drawing reference numbers.

2 While there are 136 sheets of paper, one is entirely blank and two have only outlines of panels.

3 The earliest dated drawing in this Collection is plate 2 (20 November 1874), which shows the bird arches in the Index Hall.

4 The drawing is made to what is known as 'shrinkage scale' (see Chapter V); that is, larger than full size, to be used by modellers as a full-scale drawing in wet clay, which would then shrink to the proper size as it dried and was fired.

5 British Architectural Library, Drawings Collection, Waterhouse Collection: undated detail drawing (Wat [23]) for firedogs for the Private Wing, Eaton Hall. His Grace was complaining about the over-elaborate ornament of a pair of firedogs, rather than any animal sculpture, though the particular item does carry the Westminster badge of the hound's head.

6 See Richard Owen, *A History of British Fossil Mammals and Birds*, London, 1846, fig 119.

7 Only twenty drawings bear later dates than these, which were 'sent away Apl 16/78'. The latest drawing in the collection is dated 20 December 1878, and of the twenty latest drawings, fourteen are for the principal stairs.

8 The two series are lettered A to F for the beasts and A to G for the roundels. Using capitals for the beasts and lower case for the roundels, we find, for example, the following interplay for the west wing: A a B b C c B d A a C b A c C d B a A b C c B.

9 See tracing 7203/354A, [Wat 56] in the British Architectural Library, Drawings Collection.

10 Perspective of the Natural History Museum at South Kensington, *c.*1870, British Architectural Library, Drawings Collection (temporary catalogue number: WAT [243] 1 extra.

11 This drawing was seen among the archives held in the office of the late DB Waterhouse, great grandson of Alfred Waterhouse.

12 See NHM Library & Archives, m/s index of the drawings, p6.

13 See Appendix. It is as confusing for the non-scientist as it must be infuriating for the scientist that so many of the earlier identifications have proved fallible. In this text we have stuck to the Victorian names as given on the drawings.

14 *The Building News*, 25 Oct 1878, facing p422.

15 *The Building News*, 13 Dec 1878, facing p612.

16 See Mark Girouard, *Alfred Waterhouse and the Natural History Museum*, The Natural History Museum, London, 1999, p37.

17 Similar rosettes are also cut into the woodwork of some door frames on the upper floors, giving the building a consistency of decoration in its fittings as well as in its structure.

18 This works out at sixty-six casts of each panel for piers and pilasters, the highest number of repeats of any of the major decorative pieces. (See Chapter V)

19 Professor Carla Yanni of Rutgers University has suggested to me that Waterhouse's dodo may be based not on any scientific illustration, but on the painting in the University Museum at Oxford. It was she who drew my attention to the fact that it was, in reality, probably longer necked and skinnier than in The Natural History Museum relief. (See Chapter IV)

20 This is the fourth appearance of this reptile, though only three designs survive. I believe it is the only species to appear so many times in the Museum, which suggests the interest attached to this recently identified genus of dinosaur.

21 The Spirit House to the rear of the Museum, reached from Princes Gate, was an addition of 1882, and dealt with as a separate commission. Although it uses the same buff terracotta and round arched forms, it is very much plainer than the Museum itself. Its sculptural decoration is limited to a pair of finials in the form of a cat and dog. The quality of the modelling is quite different from the work on the main building, which suggests that Waterhouse no longer had Dujardin to rely on.

22 Waterhouse regularly gave sketches to friends, and it may well be that some of these designs were dispersed in this way.

the draughtsman's contribution

It might at first seem odd that a man with no reputation as a sculptor should have been responsible for such a stunning collection of ornamental models. Yet this curious situation merely underlines the importance of the drawings. It demonstrates Waterhouse's imaginative conception and, in relation to the finished work, reveals the close partnership between the architect and his sculptor. Each drawing is not only a fine piece of pencil-work, but also a set of instructions for the sculptor, who had to turn these sketches into three-dimensional forms that must be true to the designs and effective as ornament on a richly decorative building. The quality of information provided by Waterhouse in his pencil sketches was, therefore, crucial. Yet his role in achieving this world of ornament needs to be set in the context of his role as architect of the whole Museum. In that light, his contribution to the decorative scheme as a whole involved not just the designing of the terracotta and overseeing the production of this menagerie. He also conceived and designed other forms of ornament, notably the painted ceilings, without which the museum would lose much of its character. Finally, his role in dealing with committees, whether of scientists or government paymasters, was vital in ensuring that these brilliant designs were carried through to completion. The terracotta flora and fauna, for all their unique quality, are merely the most extensive ornamental element in a larger whole.

When he won the commission for the Museum, Waterhouse's reputation was that of a talented draughtsman and a brilliant planner and constructor. So firmly has this reputation stuck that his skill in designing the terracotta ornament of the Museum is often taken for granted. Yet, in 1875, when he started to draw his specimens, he had no public reputation as an artist and was not even an Associate of the Royal Academy. His skill might have been judged by the dozen or so architectural perspectives he had already exhibited at the Academy, but only those who knew him would have been fully aware of his extraordinary talent with a pencil. From his early youth, Waterhouse had shown a flair for draughtsmanship, and the tradition is that he had initially wanted to be an artist, but adopted architecture in deference to his more practically-minded Quaker parents. However, they evidently encouraged his drawing. As soon as he began his architectural pupilage, he was busy with the first of the series of sketchbooks that he filled with fine, minute drawings in the years from 1851 to 1899. These reveal a rapidly developing ability to catch the essential elements of buildings and landscape, and to reduce them to the size of a postcard with a deft hand and a sure eye. On one tour to Germany, he squeezed on to one page half a dozen evocative images of Rhineland castles, each scarcely more than an inch square. It seems as though he was never without a sketchbook and pencil, endlessly recording with equal pains such things as the structure of a railway station roof in France, the brick cornice of a modern building in Cologne, or a picturesque farmhouse at Chagford in Devon (fig 22). This last was sketched during a spring holiday at the time he was working on the terracotta for the Museum, and amply demonstrates his free and sensitive use of the pencil.

22. A spring break in 1876, a prime year in the design work for the Museum ornament, produced this delightful pencil sketch of a farmhouse at Chagford in Devon. Waterhouse's uncanny ability to suggest form and texture with a real economy of line is abundantly evident. (SB VII, 10.5 x 16.5 cm. Private Collection)

23. Waterhouse's commitment to ornamental Gothic goes back to Ruskin, from whose *Seven Lamps of Architecture*, 1849, he traced a plate (No.IX) of Giotto's campanile in Florence in 1857. ("Scraps 2", 10.5 x 16.5 cm. Private Collection)

32   Waterhouse's architectural career, and his education in the picturesque, began with an extended tour of the Continent in 1853–4, when he was twenty-three years old. He had been sent as an articled pupil to train in the offices of Richard Lane and PB Alley in Manchester, and the earliest signed architectural drawings by him date from 1851. On his return, he presented his parents with a handsome volume in which hundreds of pages from his sketchbooks are carefully mounted, each dated, and the location recorded in minute handwriting. These drawings already show his extraordinary ability to capture the forms and textures of a whole building, or even a townscape, in the compass of a few square inches. In some of his earliest sketches, there is a facility and a delicacy of touch that is breathtaking. His topographical drawings are often enlivened with little groups of people very much in the style of Samuel Prout. Indeed, it was partly from Prout's books that Waterhouse had learned his drawing, for he had been given a copy of *Hints on Light, Shadow & Composition*[1] for his fourteenth birthday. This was one of many books of instruction, and the young Waterhouse also learned from the writings of James Duffield Harding, who had been Ruskin's drawing master.[2] It went without saying that a young architect of the 1850s would be much impressed by the work of John Ruskin, and his sketchbook for 1857; unsurprisingly, includes an image of a window of Giotto's campanile in Florence, lovingly copied from Ruskin's *Seven Lamps of Architecture* (fig 23).[3] The book was not new in 1857; indeed, the last volume of the later and better-known *Stones of Venice* had already been out for four years. Nor was Waterhouse in Italy that year, taking his holiday in Germany. So the copying of this image in 1857 demonstrates the extent of his debt to Ruskin and his perception of the picturesque and beautiful in Gothic architecture.

Waterhouse, however, was much more than a copier or recorder of interesting details, whether on his own account or from the drawings of others. When sketching, he appears to have used both his pocket sketchbooks, and larger pads (around 18 x 26 and 27 x 37 centimetres), regularly cross-referencing details in one book to larger drawings, few of which now survive.[4] It appears that he often gave away his larger sketches to friends and pupils, which makes the survival of the terracotta sketches even more miraculous. In his view, it was the looking and remembering that mattered, and his sketches were little more to him than a means to an end. But that end was not always designing buildings – increasingly, he made time to indulge his love of the picturesque in watercolour painting. Initially, this was an adjunct to his designing, and his first Royal Academy exhibit was a perspective of a new house in the Lake District that he had drawn for a client.[5] To begin with, it seems, these paintings were done strictly in a business context, and, though he exhibited almost every year from 1868 on, it was not until 1884 that he began to show topographical watercolours and picturesque landscapes. The landscape of Warkworth that he submitted that year was reckoned to be 'one of the most brilliant… watercolour drawings in an exhibition which is exceptionally strong in watercolours, even for the Academy'.[6] By then, the Museum was completed, and Waterhouse himself had been elected an Associate of the Royal Academy.[7] Yet he had started painting landscapes long before the 1880s.

Although his Academy pictures were large (often around 90 x 60 centimetres), he had regularly used his smaller sketch pads for watercolours. Of the surviving works, many of the earlier ones are pencil drawings heightened with white, in a Proutian manner, or washed with colour. But by the 1870s, he had developed into a sensitive and accomplished watercolourist. His sketch of the quarry at Tintagel (fig 24), made on a summer holiday in 1876, amply demonstrates his feeling for the dramatic viewpoint, and is executed with a freedom and sureness of touch that is more than merely mechanical. A few years earlier, in December 1873, when the designing of the Museum terra-

24. Waterhouse produced this fine sketch of the quarry landing at Tintagel during a summer vacation from his work designing at the Museum. It is eloquent testimony to his ability as an artist. (27 x 37.5 cm. Private Collection)

cotta was just beginning, he had produced the delicate view of Lake Nemi in Italy (fig 25). This work is uncharacteristic in its pale tints of pink and cream, yet these are the tones he had in mind while designing The Natural History Museum. Over the years, he produced many dozens of attractive pieces such as these, which might have been ample evidence of his ability as an artist if they had been known outside his office and his immediate circle of friends.

Waterhouse, after all, was commissioned as architect of the building, and any reputation he had as a draughtsman was for his clear and accurate architectural drawings. Such things were vastly different from fine art drawings, and much of the interest in the sketches for the terracotta of the Museum lies in the fact that they were produced neither by a naturalist nor by an artist, but by an architect. Architectural drawing required other skills and was, at least by the 1870s, a matter of team work. Literally hundreds of separate drawings were required, from site plans to structural details.[8] There were plans for different sites, and different versions of the design for the South Kensington site even before work began. Then there needed to be overall designs and details of all parts and materials; finally, any number of tracings were required for the builders. As Waterhouse himself pointed out:

"It will be needful for the proper conduct of the Works that several duplicates of the whole of the drawings should be made. I shall myself require one set for constant reference; the Clerk of Works will also require a complete set, and the Contractors must have two sets at least. The number of tracings therefore which will be required will be large so far as the Contract drawings are concerned, and irrespective of the Detail drawings for every part of the work which I have to make as the building proceeds…"[9]

There was a mountain of drawing work to be done, and the essential quality of each drawing was that it should display accurate information clearly. Waterhouse already had a reputation for doing just that. Yet it was clearly impossible for him to make all the drawings himself, and some details he may not have handled at all. His practice was to assemble a team of draughtsmen, under an office senior, to work on particular commissions. For The Natural History Museum, we know the names of no less than twenty-four draughtsmen who worked on the design between 1870 and 1876, under the most senior of the assistants, Charles Scott.

Some of the activities of the team will have involved taking measurements of the site as work progressed, and transferring these to new drawings. One or two of the draughtsmen involved, such as G W Nicolay, are known to us as perspective specialists, since Waterhouse occasionally allowed them to sign drawings. There will have been others whose task went no further than laboriously tracing the

34

25. Waterhouse's sketch of Lake Nemi in Italy, done on Christmas Eve 1873.
(19 x 28 cm. Private Collection)

drawings to the high standards of 'the gov'nor', or under the supervision of his longstanding Chief Clerk. One of the most tedious, but nonetheless essential, tasks was simply marking on each sheet the brick scale (which can be seen on the left-hand edge of figure 8, p16), recording the position of each course of the brick core. Such menial tasks might seem irrelevant to the designs of the terracotta ornament, but it should be remembered that the various plants and creatures were actually modelled on blocks of terracotta that formed a part of the structure of the Museum. Two horizontal cross sections in figure 18 (p24) show just how carefully each block – in this case the ones with fishes on them – was shaped to enclose and provide a fireproof casing for the iron stanchions that carried the structure. A further problem is that clay shrinks in drying and firing. Thus every block had to be drawn slightly oversize for it to fit precisely when manufactured. There was, in short, a great deal of drawing for the team to do. Waterhouse reckoned that he himself had spent 192 days at work on drawings and the like for the Museum; the 134 surviving sketches for the terra-cotta must have occupied a significant part of that time.

The task of designing the terracotta ornament was, therefore, only part of a much larger job of draughtsmanship, and involved co-operation with others. Even for the sketches, it is likely that Waterhouse relied on his assistants to draw out the basic shape of the block before he began his sketch. It is the detail of each relief that is the autograph work by the master; and it is the quality of that detail that makes these drawings so special. However, there are still some unusual features. Although the designs were for terracotta blocks that would have to fit precisely into a structure, none of the sketches shows a scale. Yet in designing for terracotta, Waterhouse frequently produced drawings to shrinkage scale (see fig. 3, p11). Presumably, for these models, the actual dimensions for each item were given to the sculptor from the main design drawings, and it was left to him to allow for shrinkage. Then again, given that Waterhouse had an architect's training, it is surprising that he did not choose to supply at least front and side elevations, if not plans and sections for more of his creatures. For a few of the designs, such as the bird and monkey arches (plates 1–4) he, or his assistants, did draw out a section of the basic moulding on which the terracotta ornament would be placed. For the most part, however, Waterhouse appears to have thought a single image sufficient. In that most of the decoration was in relief, this worked pretty well,

though there are one or two cases in the museum where the transference of a flat image into three-dimensional relief leaves unfortunate side views. In one panel at the foot of the great stair, for instance, the side of the ounce's neck is modelled plain with the rough fur only on the 'front' of the panel (plate 89), though the plain side view is readily visible as one mounts the stairs. This is a common problem with relief carving, which occurs even on the Parthenon frieze, but at The Natural History Museum, Waterhouse and his sculptor managed to keep such lapses to a minimum.

It was generally assumed that an architect could either design the necessary ornament for his buildings himself, or would commission appropriate sculptors. The reality was not quite so simple. Another celebrated Goth, EW Godwin, having won the competition for Northampton Town Hall in 1860 with a design that included several life-size figures on the façade, admitted that he had never before done any life drawing. He was fortunate in his partnership with the sculptor RL Boulton. Waterhouse was similarly fortunate in finding M Dujardin to make the models. It could certainly be said that Waterhouse moved in 'art' circles. He had joined a sketching club while a pupil at Manchester, and was a friend of the Manchester Pre-Raphaelite, Frederic Shields.

26. The principal doorway of the Prudential Assurance Company building, Nottingham, is crowned with heraldic date stones and a canopied figure of Prudence, modelled for Waterhouse by FW Pomeroy in 1898.

27. The Holborn façade of the Prudential building boasts a three-story oriel window with a frieze of classical cherubs at its base. These were very probably the work of FW Pomeroy, but Farmer and Brindley made the models here as they did at The Natural History Museum.

Later, we find that Sir Frederick Leighton was among the circle of friends who attended Mrs Waterhouse's dinner parties at their home in New Cavendish Street. Towards the end of his career, Waterhouse came to know, and regularly commissioned FW Pomeroy, one of the country's leading Academic sculptors, who designed the much repeated image of Prudence for the Prudential Assurance Company and probably other details as well (figs 26 & 27). However, his friendship with Hamo Thornycroft is the one most likely to have influenced him while at work on the Museum. It appears he got to know him around 1872, when the young man first exhibited at the Royal Academy; by the early 1880s he was a frequent guest at Waterhouse's country house at Yattendon. Waterhouse was certainly involved in getting the Duke of Westminster to commission his celebrated group, Artemis and her Hounds, that stood in the waiting hall at Eaton, and he was evidently much impressed by the young sculptor's talent. Thus it is possible that Waterhouse discussed with him some of the problems and potential of clay modelling; Thornycroft may even have been the one to suggest which of the modellers might do a good job for Waterhouse. There is no proof, but the linkage of interest between Waterhouse, Thornycroft and Dujardin at this period, and in the same city, does at least make some contact a possibility.

At any rate, Waterhouse found a congenial modeller in Dujardin, and was able to rely on his producing fine work from the delicate sketches. It was important that the sculptor should understand fully what was in the architect's mind, and be in sympathy with his draughtsmanship. There was a world of difference between the quality of the terracotta details as sketched at a small scale on the constructional drawings and what was needed to ensure the standard required by Waterhouse. A comparison of the cat capital sketched in figure 19 (p24) with the drawing given to the sculptor by Waterhouse (plate 120) reveals just how far Waterhouse was able to go. It also shows both how fortunate the Museum was to have so talented an artist in its designer, and how lucky Waterhouse was to find so sympathetic a craftsman in Dujardin. The amount of effort he invested in drawing them suggests that he greatly enjoyed making the designs; and equally, he obviously had complete confidence in his modeller. It is tempting to believe that Dujardin might already have had an interest in natural history, and that Waterhouse might perhaps have met him sketching in the natural history galleries of the old British Museum. The more prosaic probability is that he was already employed by the efficient firm of modellers that Waterhouse commissioned for the work. However, as the commission developed, the architect found such confidence in Dujardin's ability to turn his sketches into satisfactory models that he was able to leave him to work from a single sketch.

This argues a good deal for the sculptor, as we shall see, but is less surprising when we remember that the majority of the sculptures were in relief. Such creatures as the fish that form the base of the piers in the great southern galleries were well-suited to drawing in two dimensions. But the deeper relief and the three-dimensional figures required a high degree of understanding between architect and sculptor. Perhaps more surprising was Waterhouse's decision to supply only one sketch for the great beasts on the cornice. These were to be modelled in the round, and, being almost six feet tall, were a major feature of the façade. Yet Waterhouse provides only a side or a front view (plates 35–40). This could be because the beasts were mostly viewed from in front as the visitor approached the Museum; it is interesting to note that, in the case of the wolf and eagle finials to the gables of the Pavilions, where an angled view would be more common, he does provide both front and side views. One reason for allowing the sculptor to work from a single sketch may simply have been that Waterhouse was determined that he alone should make the sketches, and the sheer amount of work involved precluded his producing more than one drawing for each

28. Detail of the roof of the east wing with seated *Mylodon*, gargoyle and *Xiphodon* in the the roundel of the gable (see plate 39 & 29).

piece. In any case, he was careful to oversee the second stage of the work, ensuring that the three-dimensional models were approved before they were sent to the manufacturers. In one letter, he expressed his concern that they should be seen and approved by Owen himself before being manufactured.[10]

This careful handling of the Superintendent of the new Museum might have been simply due to the fact that Owen was a prickly character, or the result of difficulty in drawing convincing extinct creatures. Yet the sort of attention to detail implied is typical of Waterhouse and there is plenty of evidence that he was concerned to get the highest quality in order to please his clients. As early as 1871, he had written to the Chief Commissioner of Works, when the

design was going to competitive tender, to say:

"In preparing the Specification of the work it is necessary to consider with especial care that part of it which relates to the Terra Cotta. I beg to submit to you that the right way of dealing with the question will be to procure, in the first place, Estimates from several of the best contractors, not with a view to the whole of the Terra Cotta being placed with any one firm but divided between two or three whose Estimates are most favourable. As a preliminary step I beg to apply for permission to get models prepared for certain portions of the work: Such models to be cast in plaster and duplicates sent to each Terra Cotta maker invited to tender. From such models the various manufacturers would be able, without much trouble to prepare samples of

29. Simple capitals and twisted shafts together with voussoirs with patterned soffits make a rich entrance to the house Waterhouse designed for Thomas Fowell Buxton at Easneye near Ware in 1867.

38   the actual work required and they should be required to do so and submit them with their tenders".[11]

Of course, such a letter only indicates that Waterhouse was an efficient architect, which was the chief reason for his being commissioned in the first place. It was also the case that he had a passionate interest in ornament, particularly in the richness of geometrical decoration. One should not ignore the importance of the many simple blocks that create patterns by repetition and alternation (fig 28). The frequent reiteration of a simple chevron band above the capitals of the galleries (plates 114 & 120) and elsewhere in the building, is typical of the way in which Waterhouse set about achieving a unity in his rich ornamental scheme. It even occurs on the piers of the boundary railing. The sketches of baluster shafts with abstract patterns are as lovingly drawn as any of the exotic beasts, and were probably more familiar ground for him. He had already developed a rich decorative ornamental vocabulary in buildings such as the Assize Courts in Manchester, which effectively made his reputation. Even in more modest commissions, such as the mansion he built for Thomas Fowell Buxton at Stanstead Abbots, he had mastered the art of repeating simple patterns to make a rich doorway (fig 29).

The fact that terracotta could be modelled so effectively to produce bold, decorative shapes was something that clearly fascinated Waterhouse. The Natural History Museum was not quite the first major commission on which he used the material (fig 30), but it certainly allowed him to explore it to the full. For the rest of his career he was to use this facing material so extensively that he became known as Mr Terra Cotta. Throughout his career, he lost no opportunity to enrich his designs with boldly modelled features in coloured clay, which could enhance the richness of each structure at very little extra cost (figs 31–33). He also understood very well the importance of picturesque forms, even in relatively simple buildings, and loved features such as oriel windows set at angles across corners. Later, he was to discover how effective the large blocks of terracotta could be for corbelling out such features (fig 34). But The Natural History Museum demanded more than mere geometrical games, and here, Waterhouse's training in the Gothic style may have stood him in good stead. An early commission for a bank at Leighton Buzzard had given him the opportunity to devise some lively ornamental beasts to be carved in stone (fig 35). He was also at work in Manchester, where he designed some attractive capitals with dragons and foliage combined (fig 37). But these were nothing compared to the richness of animal ornament called for at the Museum, and it is a tribute to his ability and imagination as an artist that he was able to create such a varied menagerie in so short a period.

30. Waterhouse's first major commission for terracotta was for the lining and vaulting ribs of the passages of Manchester Town Hall begun in 1868.

31. The simplest of red Ruabon terracotta contrasted with a darker brick enriched the side of Waterhouse's Liverpool Royal Infirmary of 1887–90.

32. An exaggerated frame in red terracotta makes a dramatic feature out of a small ground-floor doorway in the Victoria building of Liverpool University (1887–92).

40

33. Above: Repeated cusped arches frame the upper office windows in one block of the Prudential headquarters in Holborn.

34. Right: Terracotta blocks are used to corbel out dramatic corner turrets at University College Hospital, a design by Waterhouse of 1896.

35. Below: Waterhouse, as an architect of the Gothic Revival had a long experience of ornamental carving such as this animal on a bank in Leighton Buzzard from 1865.

36. Below right: An ornate triple pillar in Ste Croix at Bordeaux, sketched in April 1873, is undoubtedly a source for the many varieties of shafts Waterhouse produced for the Museum. (SB VI, 10.5 x 16.5 cm. Private Collection)

41

37. Foliage and dragons make a dramatic capital in the vestibule of Waterhouse's Manchester Town Hall, carved in Spinkwell stone by Farmer and Brindley, c. 1873.

Waterhouse's training as a Gothic Revival designer also led him to be constantly on the lookout for relevant details. A visit to Bordeaux in 1873, for instance, showed him patterned shafts in Ste Croix, which can be seen as inspiration for the shafts of his great portal at the Museum (fig 36). However, Waterhouse seldom simply collected precedents that could be carefully copied on his buildings. Instead, he preferred to master the principles of the medieval designers and adapt their solutions, often many years after he had first seen them, when faced with similar problems himself. Thus the pattern of an arcade seen at Andernach in 1861 may well have helped him work out the arcading of the Index Museum, and a set of capitals with lively beasts crawling through foliage could have given a hint as to how to manage the larger capitals of the entrance and of the Index Museum (fig 38). Only very occasionally do we find details in his sketchbooks that are directly reproduced in his own work and even then he avoided actual copying (fig 39, and plate 1). The important thing for him as a designer was to bring his own creative ingenuity and imagination to bear on the problem at hand.

There was a further contribution that he was able to make to the ornament of the Museum. It is well known that he had a hard time steering the commission through the various changes of government and alternating enthusiasm and parsimony of the various First Commissioners of Works. That the eventual building was achieved with so little loss of richness is a tribute to his persistence and perhaps confirms the tradition that his smile was worth a thousand pounds a year. It is entirely conceivable that one reason for his choice of terracotta as the facing material was that the material was also structural. The ornament could hardly be rejected as an extravagant extra! However, for Waterhouse and Owen, it seems that the terracotta was

only one element in an overall scheme of decoration that was to spread to ceilings as well as walls. Sadly, no drawings survive for the painted ceilings, though they are outstanding examples of a type of decoration that rarely survives. At the Museum, they very nearly failed to materialise. When Waterhouse was first required to cut the cost of the building, he wrote to Ayrton, the economising First Commissioner, to confirm that 'the painting on the plastering and all the decorative painting have now been omitted' and the sentence is firmly marked with a double line of blue government chalk.[12] It was not enough and Ayrton wrote back demanding a reduction of £83,000 on the tender of £395,000 and suggesting nine possible economies. These included reductions in height and the use of brick instead of terracotta for the rear elevation, which was in fact done. But the most damaging demands were the substitution of a plain brick wall for the proposed boundary and a plaster ceiling instead of wooden in the Index Museum. Worst of all was the demand to use Portland stone for the façade 'omitting intricate detailed ornament', to omit 'all figures of animals on the parapets' and the substitution of 'plaster for terra cotta inside the buildings'.[13] The Museum would have been plain indeed and though details of the argument do not survive, Waterhouse certainly deserves great credit for making enough economies to allow the retention of the terracotta.

There was some support for better decoration once construction began. Henry Cole, the *éminence grise* of the South Kensington Museums, wrote to the First Commissioner arguing for mosaic and tile floors: 'On the superior decorative effect of Mosaics and Tiles there can be no second opinion among all having any sense of beauty. The most stately public buildings both ancient and modern use them.'[14] But the Museum never acquired elaborately patterned floors, Waterhouse rightly judging that it was better to accept the stringency for the time being. He had, after all, retained his beloved terracotta for all the

42

38. Sketches of capitals in the Cathedral at Andernach, Switzerland, done in September 1861, may have given Waterhouse some general ideas for the capitals of The Natural History Museum; and his analysis of the arcade could have informed the treatment of the galleries in the Index Museum. (SB III. 37, 10.5 x 16.5 cm. Private Collection)

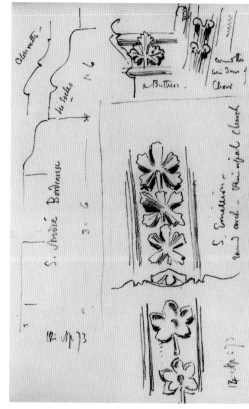

39. Waterhouses sketchbooks provide very few exact precedents for his designs for the Museum. This sketch of running foliage from the principal church in St Emillion, done in April 1873, is uncannily like the foliage of the bird arches in the Index Museum (See plates 1 & 2). (SB VI, 10.5 x 16.5 cm. Private Collection)

40. Panel from the ceiling of the Index Museum painted by Charles James Lea: (*Quercus robur*) the oak (The Natural History Museum, Picture Library).

44

41. Panel from the ceiling of the Index Museum painted by Charles James Lea: (*Pinus sylvestris*) the Scotch pine (The Natural History Museum, Picture Library).

42. Panel from the ceiling of the Index Museum painted by Charles James Lea: (*Ficus carica*) the wild fig (The Natural History Museum, Picture Library).

43. Panel from the ceiling of the Index Museum painted by Charles James Lea: (*Amygdalus persica*) the almond (The Natural History Museum, Picture Library).

45. Ceiling of the lobby to the Refreshment Room on the first floor with stencilled paterae and birds, dragonflies, butterflies and bees (The Natural History Museum, Picture Library).

44. One bay of the Index Museum ceiling.

public surfaces of the building. Later, he was to reinstate at least some painted ceilings by what seems very close to a ruse, claiming that the decoration, if ordered at once, could represent a saving. He wrote again to the First Commissioner in 1878, when the work was drawing to a close:

"It appears to me to be a matter of importance that the plaster panels of the Ceilings in the Index Museum, at South Kensington, shall receive at the present time a certain amount of decoration in colour. I am of opinion that the effect of these important sections of the new buildings would be greatly enhanced thereby, and the work could be done at the present time at far less expense than at a later period, when the place will have been cleared of scaffolding. I estimate the cost of decorating the panels in question at Seven hundred pounds…"[15]

Agreement was not automatic, for Waterhouse had to write again arguing that the painting had originally been designed in colour and gold, and cost £1,800, but 'at the request of the First Commissioner this provision was entirely omitted from the specification'.[16] However, the government seems by then to have become resigned to going ahead, and the result was a further important element in the overall decoration of the Museum.

The painting was undertaken by the firm of Best & Lea, who had already done work for Waterhouse at Pilmore Hall

near Darlington. They were also employed by him at Eaton Hall and Manchester Town Hall, and a little later he was to call on them again for Pembroke College, Cambridge, and for at least three more of his country houses. He evidently thought highly of their work, for he commissioned them to decorate the ceiling of the library in his own mansion at Yattendon in Berkshire. They may well have received yet more commissions from Waterhouse, but their work is not yet researched, and few drawings survive. Sadly, not a single sketch, still less any full-size drawings, survive for the two great schemes at The Natural History Museum. One cartoon from Yattendon survives, drawn by Charles James Lea. It was undoubtedly he who drew out the full-size cartoons that must have been used in The Natural History Museum, but Waterhouse will have provided him with designs, presumably similar to those he made for Dujardin. The plant panels match the rest of Waterhouse's work too closely to be by another hand and it is inconceivable that, having carefully designed every terracotta plant and animal, he would have delegated the design of a ceiling.

Lea differed from Dujardin in being both an artist and a partner in his own firm. Whether the resulting status gave him extra freedom is unclear, and the lack of information in the Museum archives leaves this element of the decoration still shrouded in mystery. Only a few letters in the Public Record Office hint at the development of the scheme, which is itself as rare and important as it is attractive. The only sketches we know of by Waterhouse are referred to in a letter to the Secretary of the Office of Works:

"The first sketches of the proposed work I beg to submit to you herewith but every part will involve careful reconsideration on the spot. I beg to suggest whether it would not be the most satisfactory course for me to get one panel painted, in the first instance, and then to ask the First Commissioner's approval of the treatment, before proceeding farther?"[17]

46   One would love to know what sort of sketch was submitted. It was clearly vital that the government should feel they were in full control, and that Waterhouse was not indulging in any extravagance. The sample panel, or apparently two samples, evidently were painted, for they are referred to in the specification. Waterhouse had written in May; by July, Best & Lea were able to tender for painting the 'ceilings of galleries and staircases, also to waggon headed ceilings in lobbies at ends of gallery, gallery ceiling between Index Museum and British Natural History Museum, also recesses at east and west on Ground floor of Index Museum and entirely round British Natural History Museum'.[18] Fortunately, their tender (apparently a separate sum for the Index Museum) came well within the £700 allowance at £585. But Waterhouse's hint of reconsideration on the spot, and the question of the freedom he allowed Charles James Lea is raised immediately by a second specification submitted on the same date to:

"Select and prepare drawings of fruits and flowers most suitable and paint and gild same in upper panels of roof in a similar manner to the Pomegranate and Magnolia now done as specimens. All the lower panels to be further enriched by the fruit and flowers (as the case may be) being gilded and glazed down in appropriate tones as now shown in the 'Orange' and 'Apple' panels in the first bays."[19]

This description makes it clear that the basic scheme of the Index Museum was settled, but that Waterhouse and Lea had decided that the main panels were not rich enough. Once again, Waterhouse was able to persuade the government to stretch their permission, for Best & Lea were asking a further £150 for this. Waterhouse, naturally, supported their estimate as strongly as he could and by August was able to write that 'Messrs Best & Lea… are now very efficiently carrying out the work already sanctioned'. He also slipped in a mention that £1,435 had already been authorised, and Best & Lea were now offering to do all the ceilings for £1,975, a figure that accords suspiciously well with the £1,800 that Waterhouse claimed was cut from the original budget back in 1872. The result was the extraordinary painted forest that roofs the Index Museum and all the other painted ceilings that complement the terracotta so well.

What Waterhouse and Lea created is a series of panels illustrating trees and plants that form the most extensive flower decoration in the Museum. The Index Museum was lit from the side and above in a way deemed ideal for displaying its contents; that was after all the aim. The glazing left a solid centre of the roof to be panelled and painted. Each of the six bays of the ceiling is decorated with carefully identified depictions of plants and trees (figs 40–43). Each bay is divided into nine compartments, and with the three narrower but similar bays of the Entrance Hall, made a total of 162 panels. There was no attempt to fill the entire set with 162 different plants, a course of action that would probably have rendered the appearance chaotic. Instead, Waterhouse distinguished the different viewpoints. The narrower panels of the Entrance Hall are seen most effectively from the upper flight of stairs or from the second floor – that is, from close to – and they are supplied with nine different plants, each carefully identified with its Latin name, for every bay of nine panels. In the Index Museum, there are two types of image. The upper ones, furthest from the viewer, are smaller in area within their panels, the jump in size concealed by a patterned border. Significantly, they are not identified. However, each group of six lower panels, seen from sixty feet below, is filled with a single design, again with its Latin name beneath. In both the Index Museum and Entrance Hall the lower panels are painted over a cream ground and the upper over green, which gives a unity to the whole complex space, but also makes a darker band and emphasises the shadows along the roof ridge.

The plants themselves are depicted in muted greens and greys, with touches of red, though it is impossible to tell how far they may have been dulled by a century of gaslight, dust and smoke. However, the more dramatic contrast of the gold in which the fruits are picked out against the dark green of the upper panels suggest that muted tints were probably the architect's intention from the start. It would have been characteristic of both the man and his age. Also typical of Waterhouse, and of the compromise path he followed at the Museum, is the way the growth of the different species is depicted. All twelve are virtually identical in the way a single stem rises in the central panel and divides neatly into smaller twigs to fill the outer five. These are far from being depictions of entire trees, but should be read as typical outer branches; the relative scale of leaf and twig only makes sense on that supposition. This system also had the advantage of allowing the depiction of individual leaves for clearer identification. Additionally, it meant that the branches could be depicted in a more two-dimensional manner that would not disrupt the flat ceiling panels or conflict with the solidity of the terracotta.

The decoration of this extraordinary roof is completed by the provision of sets of formalised foliage, a total of six different designs in gilt filigree ironwork that fill the triangular bracing of the light iron arches supporting it (fig 44). There are twenty-two such triangles, and the iron patterns repeat, beginning alternately from left and right, on each of the five arches of the Index Museum, an ornamental feature that is barely noticeable among the rest of the decorative wealth. Finally, at the ends of the galleries are lobbies to the Refreshment Room, and here again, Waterhouse managed to secure painted ceilings. Each space has a series of panels, delicately stencilled with birds and bees, butterflies and dragonflies, scattered among a variety of paterae, all in cream on a pale blue background. The same insects appear, though probably to a different scale, in gold on the ceiling panels of the Index Museum (fig 45).

The theme of floral painting was continued in the Museum of British Natural History (now the Waterhouse Café), which is a smaller version of the Index Museum. As has been seen, it was a space in which Waterhouse was unable to introduce much in the way of terracotta ornament, but he was clearly determined that it should also have some special character. He therefore repeated the recipe of the Index Museum, but with a variation. The ceiling is in blocks of six panels instead of nine, smaller and closer to the viewer than that in the Index Museum. So instead of dividing it into two bands, Waterhouse used the deep green ground on all the panels. The lower row has portraits of British wild flowers, set within patterned borders and picked out in blue, brown and dun with gold for petals and seed pods (figs 46–48). Beneath each flower, and easily legible, is its Latin name, continuing the more determinedly educational approach of the Index Museum. The space, slightly overshadowed by that hall, one bay to the south, tends to be dim. Waterhouse's choice of a dark colour for the ground enhances this quality, but the glitter of artificial light on the gold petals gives a vibrancy to the decoration that is not found in the other spaces. Probably the original intention had been to extend similar forms of painted decoration and botanical symbolism to the south galleries. If so, the scheme had been obediently surrendered to the First Commissioner, though each gallery, like the Museum of British Natural History, does have its own individual pattern of foliage tendrils neatly stencilled in

gold on black or red, or red and pale tints on buff, applied to the exposed undersides of the iron beams. For today's taste it is enough, providing an attractive touch of colour.

The boldness of his conception and the sheer confidence in commissioning it from Charles James Lea in the face of a parsimonious government is a final example of the contribution that Waterhouse made to the decoration of the Museum as a whole. All the constructional draughtsmanship, all the supervision of manufacturers and contractors (itself not without real problems) as well as the decoration in these additional materials, has to be set alongside the modelled terracotta as integral to his achievement. It hardly needs repeating that it is a considerable one and the dates of some of the sketches (24 December for instance), reveal that Waterhouse worked himself and his staff hard. However, it is also certain that he relished the creation of what would obviously be one of the great works of his career. He managed to satisfy the paymasters with his economy as well as providing the sort of Cathedral of Science dreamt of by Richard Owen. And if Waterhouse's contribution to the ornament was the principal one, Owen's was far from unimportant. The final building was the fruit of a unique collaboration between architect and scientist, with the support of a talented sculptor. We now need to examine this relationship and the way in which the drawings were turned into three-dimensional terracotta.

47

48

46. Flower panel from the ceiling of the Museum of British Natural History painted by Charles James Lea; (*Digitalis purpurea*) the common foxglove (The Natural History Museum, Picture Library).

48. Flower panel from the ceiling of the Museum of British Natural History painted by Charles James Lea; (*Inula helenium*) elecampane (The Natural History Museum, Picture Library).

47. Flower panel from the ceiling of the Museum of British Natural History painted by Charles James Lea; (*Rosa canina*) the dog rose (The Natural History Museum, Picture Library).

Notes

1 Samuel Prout, *Hints on Light, Shadow and Composition etc. as applicable to Landscape for Juvenile Enquirers*, Ackerman, London, 1838. His copy is inscribed 'Alfred Waterhouse Jun. In remembrance of a short but very pleasant tour in Wales on his birthday 1844'.

2 See in particular JD Harding, *The Principles & Practice of Art*, London, 1845, several pages from which were copied by Waterhouse into his first study book (Scraps, 1848, Private Collection).

3 John Ruskin, *The Seven Lamps of Architecture*, Smith Elder, London, 1849. The image is copied from plate IX, which faces the opening on the Lamp of Beauty on p94.

4 We know this because his sketchbook for 1855 records a whole day spent at St Ouen in Rouen, though it contains only one small sketch. For a comparison of the various sizes and their typical contents, see Colin Cunningham & Prudence Waterhouse, *Alfred Waterhouse 1830–1905: Biography of a Practice*, OUP, Oxford, 1992, figs 11–15.

5 See ibid., plate 16. The house is Fawe Park, near Kendal, and was exhibited at the Academy in 1857 under the anonymous title of *Cottage Erecting in Cumbria*. The client was James Bell, MP, Secretary of the RIBA.

6 *The Building News*, 1884, p817.

7 His election came in 1878, and his Diploma work was a large perspective of Manchester Town Hall, another of his greatest achievements, completed in that year. It was also the year in which he won the Gold Medal of the RIBA.

8 The largest number of surviving drawings, almost 300 sheets, are held in the Drawings Collection of the RIBA. A few are kept in the Museum, and a number of detail tracings are maintained with government papers in the Public Record Office at Kew. The office numbering sequence makes it plain that there were more drawings. Each sheet for a given commission was numbered in sequence, and the highest number among the surviving sheets is 591. Since tracings were not given a separate number but distinguished by a letter suffix (a, b, c, d, etc), it is easy to get an idea of the sheer quantity of sheets prepared.

9 PRO Work 17 16/3. Ms letter AW to First Commissioner 17 Dec 1872. Waterhouse was applying, unsuccessfully it seems, for permission to have the contract drawings copied by lithography. In a further letter (PRO Work 17 16/3.29 Jan 1873), he revealed that one set of Contract drawings alone amounted to 86 sheets.

10 See page 61

11 PRO Work 17 16/3. Ms letter from AW to First Commissioner of Works, 20 Nov 1871.

12 PRO Work 17 16/3. Ms letter AW to First Commissioner, 12 Aug 1872.

13 PRO Work 17 16/3. Office of Works Memorandum, 16 Sep 1872.

14 PRO Work 17 16/3. Ms letter from Henry Cole to First Commissioner, 26 Nov 1873.

15 PRO Work 17 18/6. Ms letter AW to Secretary, Office of Works, 26 Mar 1878. Waterhouse pointed out that he had managed to make various, unspecified, savings in the cost so far; but there is no indication of the basis for his estimate of £700 for the remarkable painted ceilings. A marginal note, signed HAH, remarks 'It seems in every way desirable that the proposed decoration should be done before the scaffolding should be removed', and recommends sanctioning the £700.

16 PRO Work 17 18/6. Ms letter AW to Secretary, Office of Works, 16 April 1878.

17 PRO Work 17 18/6. Ms letter AW to Secretary, Office of Works, 20 May 1878.

18 PRO Work 17 18/6 A7737. Tender from Messrs. Best & Lea, 4 July 1878.

19 PRO Work 17 18/6 A7737. Specification and Estimate, Best & Lea, 4 July 1878.

IV
the scientist's contribution

Waterhouse's influence is obvious everywhere in the building he created, but the greatest credit for the setting up of the institution must go to Richard Owen. The relative role of the two men in the decorative scheme, however, is difficult to disentangle. A few business letters and a handful of comments in the standard biographies of Owen are almost all we have to go on. It is likely that, with an architect regularly visiting the site, and a client who must surely have done the same, a certain amount of the discussion would have been verbal and informal. Waterhouse's office in New Cavendish Street was little more than ten minutes walk from Owen's at the British Museum, and it would have been entirely normal for architect and client, to meet and discuss the plans, chat about details of the ornament or to look over the sketches. Sadly, not one such meeting is recorded.

If we have to speculate on the likely content of unrecorded meetings, we may also extrapolate from the social context, in which the two men moved, to fill out a picture of their various interests and the ways in which these might have influenced decisions about the ornament of the Museum. In the multi-layered society of mid-Victorian London, the two men were not far apart. By the time they met, Owen, the older man, was an academic and distinguished scholar, but his background as a Lancastrian and a surgeon gave him no more status than his architect, the son of a wealthy Liverpool cotton merchant. Both were members of the professional middle classes. Owen had links with the established church and with the academic world, especially at Oxford and had been busy building connections with the aristocracy and with government. Waterhouse had links with the worlds of banking and commerce and with the law, through which he also had contact with government and the Whig aristocracy. Both lived in London. It would have been surprising if they had not met, even had there been no building commission to bring them together. I have, therefore, felt justified in expanding what is already well known about Owen's involvement with the Museum by some speculation about possible contacts in order to suggest the role he may have played in the decoration of his building.

It was Owen who first conceived the idea of a separate museum to house the natural history collections in the British Museum, and he who fought it through committees for ten years before his architect was commissioned. He had to suffer both criticism of his ideas as 'crazy and extravagant' and the disappointment of the death of his first architect, Captain Francis Fowke. Yet throughout the period from his first report in 1859[1] until construction began in 1873, he stuck to his concept of a great scientific and educational institution. More than that, he stuck to his idea of a building laid out with an Index Museum at its core and a lecture theatre and study galleries as supporting spaces, sketching this out in plan form as early as 1862. When Waterhouse finally drew the plans that were accepted, the bulk of Owen's concept survived and was encapsulated in the eventual building.

Clearly, then, Owen was concerned with more than just the idea of a scientific institution. He was deeply interested in the way the Collection would be housed. His role in the terracotta ornament is more problematic. He was in any case a scientist and not an artist. For the most part, it was his practice to commission professionals, such as George Scharf or Joseph Wolf, to produce images of specimens to his direction. It was expected of a natural scientist that he should be able to make accurate records of specimens, but the tradition of artistic illustration was probably less common in Owen's line, palaeontology, than in such areas as field botany. Owen certainly did draw specimens himself (fig 49), and was well able to record them accurately in watercolour. However, his draughtsmanship was of a different order from Waterhouse's. He preferred to work in outline in an altogether drier manner, since he was making a scientific record rather than depicting forms, still less composing patterns. His interest, too, was in fossils, fragments and skeletons, whereas Waterhouse needed to produce images of musculature and complete creatures in convincing poses.

It was, however, Owen who suggested that it would be an attractive idea to have the museum ornamented externally with images of what was displayed inside. His son records him as saying: 'I took the liberty to suggest that many objects of natural history might afford subjects for architectural ornament; and at Mr Waterhouse's request I transmitted numerous figures of such as seemed suitable for that

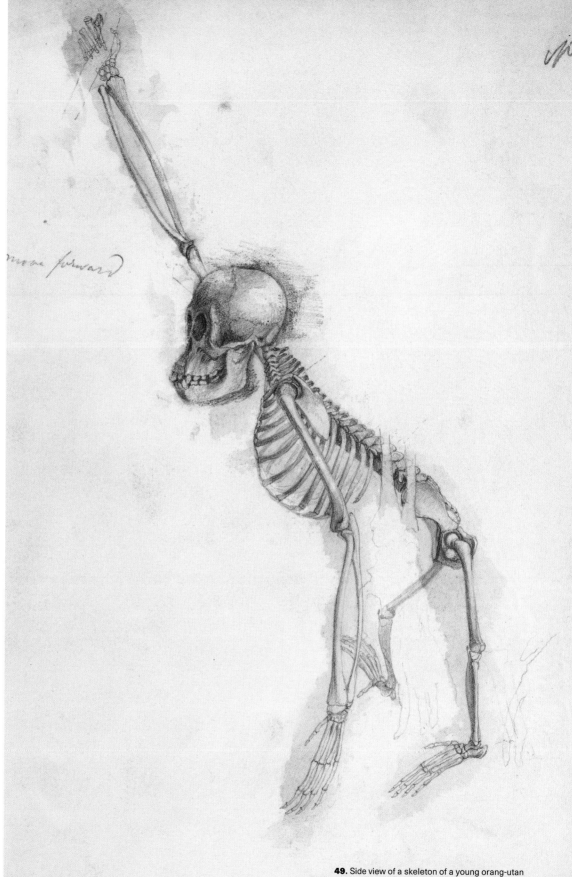

49. Side view of a skeleton of a young orang-utan
(*Simia satyrus*), n.d., signed 'R O del' (17.5 x 25.5 cm.)
with note by upper arm 'more forward' and 'No6',
noted as an illustration for *Transactions of the
Zoological Society* Vol.I, 1835, pl.XLIX, from: *The
Richard Owen Collection of Palaeontological and
Zoological Drawings* (The Natural History Museum,
Picture Library), Folio 234 c.

50. *Pezophaps solitaria* (male), n.d., signed 'R.O.del.'
(15.5 x 24 cm) Sketch of a skeleton of a dodo from:
The Richard Owen Collection of Palaeontological
and Zoological Drawings (The Natural History
Museum, Picture Library), Folio 512 c.

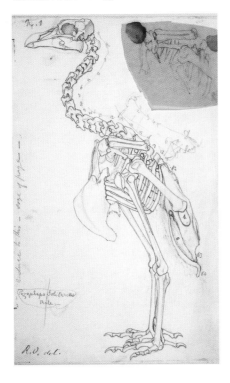

52

51. Head of a dodo, monochrome wash drawing,
n.d., unsigned (27 x 20 cm) with note: 'See Strickland
& Melville's "Dodo" - (1848). Pl. V. Sig, 2. Side view of
head of Dodo from Ashmolean Museum', from *The
Richard Owen Collection of Palaeontological and
Zoological Drawings* (The Natural History Museum,
Picture Library), Folio 512 b.

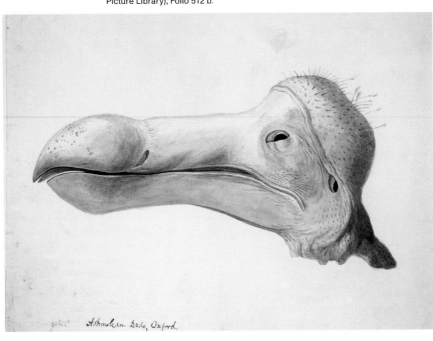

purpose'.[2] Unfortunately, it has proved all but impossible
to determine precisely what those 'numerous figures' may
have been, and there is very little evidence of exactly how
far Owen went in advising and supervising what Waterhouse produced. His own collection of drawings was substantial[3] and he might have drawn on it for suitable illustrations. However, there are problems with this theory. The
famous dodo panel (plate 127), for instance, appears to be
based on the well-known painting in Oxford, an engraving
of which was in the Owen collection. However, the collection also included other images of the species that Owen
would almost certainly have felt more reliable. One of his
own sketches of the skeleton of a dodo might have been
used as the basis for a reconstruction, and shows a much
skinnier bird with a long neck (fig 50). He also had a
detailed watercolour sketch of a dodo's head (fig 51) that
suggests a longer beak and flatter form than the one
Waterhouse drew.

It is entirely possible that he was reluctant to lend the
architect original drawings. In which case, one has to consider the plethora of published illustrations that might
have been available, either from the personal libraries of
the various departmental keepers, or from the library of
the British Museum itself, in Bloomsbury. Owen's own pub-
lications, however, would not neces-
sarily have been the most fruitful
source. His *History of British Fossil
Mammals and Birds* (1846) included
an outline of the palaeotherium,
which may very well have been the
source for Waterhouse's version in
one of the roundels of the façade
(plate 30).[4] However, Owen's interest in osteology and in the scientific
reconstruction of species from fossil
remains, meant that many of his
images are of skeletons only, and
often only of individual bones.

It would be impossible to pin-
point with any certainty other book
illustrations that might have been
selected. However, one particularly
strong candidate is the *Zoology of the
Voyage of HMS Beagle*, the publication
of which had been overseen by Owen
himself.[5] Five handsome volumes,

with a text partly by Charles Darwin and Captain Robert Fitzroy and partly by other specialists, were handsomely illustrated with images of the various orders described. Volume III part IV, on fish, contains a number of images such as that of the scorpion fish (fig 20, p25) that are broadly similar to those Waterhouse drew for the piers in the galleries, but there are no precise matches. A slightly closer parallel is found in the image of the Chilean lizard in Part III (fig 52), which shows a texture similar to that drawn by Waterhouse for the heads of his lizards on the façade (plate 54), but the parallel is still not very close, and the book shows a much more delicate creature. The fact that the drawing was by Owen's protégé, Benjamin Waterhouse Hawkins, might have made this image more interesting to Owen, but the case is far from convincing. There is, however, one image that is echoed quite closely in one of Waterhouse's drawings. His roundel of the rhea (plate 98) bears a remarkable likeness to the fine coloured lithograph of the *Rhea darwinii* in the *Zoology of the Voyage of HMS Beagle* (fig 53). What could have been more natural than that Owen should direct Waterhouse to these five volumes and their series of almost 200 plates? However, all that can really be certain is that Waterhouse must have looked to the scientists for information on the forms of a good many creatures that will have been unfamiliar to him.

Waterhouse was certainly reluctant to go ahead with models that Owen had not seen and approved. But that was hardly surprising since Waterhouse was an architect and not a scientist. Indeed, there is no evidence that he even shared the common Victorian hobby of collecting natural history specimens on holiday, and his sketchbooks include very few drawings of animals. As an added difficulty, there was little general knowledge of the forms of extinct creatures in the 1870s. The very term 'dinosaur' had only been coined in 1842 by Owen himself.[6] Waterhouse will certainly have needed Owen's advice on the forms of the extinct species. It has been shown that his pterodactyl (plate 28) is based on a detail of one of the large posters designed by Benjamin Waterhouse Hawkins (fig 54), and that it was Owen who pointed him in the direction the image.[7] However, Owen, as a scientist, will have been fully aware that a number of different species of pterodactyl were known, whereas Waterhouse's models can only be regarded as generic images. The same is true of most of the other species, which Owen is likely to have suggested for inclusion. Yet there is no clear picture of a forceful scientist

imposing a detailed scheme on a compliant architect. The story, I believe, is more complex and the relationship more fluid.

When the Museum eventually opened, it was described as 'ornamented – if so it may be termed – both externally and internally with incorrect and grotesque representations of animals, the style of the building being more adapted for a suburban tea-garden than a national museum'.[8] This was far from the sort of encomium a distinguished scientist might desire for the crowning achievement of his career. And there were other more damaging criticisms. An article in *Nature* of 1882, presenting a considered critique of the building, drew attention to the incongruity between the style (Waterhouse called it 'the round-arched style so common in Southern Germany late in the twelfth century'[9]) and the objects of the building, and described the elaborate internal decoration as a serious mistake.[10] It has also been shown that the decision to divide the collections into living and extinct species, and to decorate the building to reflect this was, as *The Daily News* gleefully reported, 'a classification not easy to reconcile perhaps with many existing theories'.[11]

Owen's position in the world of science will have had an overall influence on the decoration, and he was clearly marked as the older generation. His creationist interpretation of the world, in the decades after the publication of *On the Origin of Species* (1859), was pointed out as famously out of date. Certainly it is true that Owen was an old-fashioned scientist when compared with energetic Thomas Huxley, who is generally taken as the voice of the new science and was established in his laboratory in what is now the Henry Cole Wing of the Victoria & Albert Museum by the time Waterhouse was drawing his sketches. Much has been made of the rivalry between Owen and Huxley, especially of the latter's impatience at Owen's vacillation over Darwin's theory. Huxley may very well have made time to visit the works, and will have known in any case how Owen planned to dispose the collections. He was certainly not afraid of voicing his criticisms and it is quite possible that Waterhouse knew his views and may even have taken them into account, for, by 1881, Huxley was emphatically the leading scientist of his age. Adrian Desmond has called him the High Priest of Evolution, and his distaste for Owen and his theories was well known. If so, one could argue that the extent to which Waterhouse departed from a rigid division between living and extinct species, and from precise depiction of species

52. *Proctotretus chilensis* natural size (approximately 15 x 17 cm) Drawn from nature by B Waterhouse Hawkins on stone in Lithotint C Hullmandel's patent, from *Zoology of the Voyage of HMS Beagle under the command of Captain Fitzroy, R.N., during the years 1832-1836*, London, Smith Elder, Vol. III, Part III, Reptiles, 1842, plate 1 (The Natural History Museum, Picture Library)

54. Illustration of a pterodactyl by Benjamin Waterhouse Hawkins detail from one of a series of wall posters of *Dinosauria, or Gigantic Lizards, and Pterosauria, or Winged Lizards, that lived during the Secondary Period of the Earth's History* commissioned by the Department of Science & Art, *c.*1862. (The Natural History Museum Picture Library)

53. *Rhea darwinii* (31 x 24 cm) from *Zoology of the Voyage of HMS Beagle under the command of Captain Fitzroy, R.N., during the years 1832-1836* London, Smith Elder, Vol. II, Part II, Birds, 1841, plate XLVII, published under the supervision of Richard Owen, may be compared to Waterhouse's sketch of the rhea for one of the gallery roundels (plate 98) (The Natural History Museum, Picture Library)

in static terracotta, was a reflection of his uncertainty as to Owen's theories. Equally, one should acknowledge that Owen's views on the matter did alter in the years from 1862, when he first sketched his design, to 1881, when the Museum opened. The problem was that the arrangement of the departments and the plan of the Museum were fixed from the moment construction began, and were thus, inevitably, ten years out of date by the time it was completed. In the scientific argument, history proved Huxley the winner, rendering the creationism of the Museum's terracotta scientifically unacceptable. Owen retired in 1884, barely three years after his Museum opened. Now it is fash-

55. A view of one of the three of the monkey arches of the Index Museum and Entrance Hall.

55

ionable to lay the incongruities of the ornamental scheme at his door, as though he were himself like the dodo that adorns its walls.

It is certainly true that Owen had been slow to accept Darwin's theories, and his rigid distinction between living and extinct species could not accommodate a continuing process of evolution. And if the vilification of Owen was a popular sport in the 1870s and 1880s, it has to be admitted that there were problems with his Museum. However, we need to distinguish here between functional weaknesses and scientific incongruity in the ornament. Use very quickly showed that there were some drawbacks with the design of the Museum, and a number of modifications were made during construction, but a radical redesign was impossible, and there is no suggestion that it was even considered. However, one should remember that there were relatively few precedents for such a structure, and even the famous Oxford University Museum had been criticised on similar grounds.[12] The Natural History Museum had to satisfy the requirements not only of Owen and the government but also of the whole body of departmental curators. Waterhouse's designs might offer sufficiently varied accommodation to keep that disparate group happy, but he could never provide effectively for developments in science that had yet to be made. On the other hand, the scheme of ornament, which was to be applied to the whole building, was a major unifying element and needed to have an overall consistency. That consistency was, I believe, something with which Waterhouse was deeply concerned, while there is no evidence that Owen even considered it. Yet it seems that there was a tendency, as soon as a problem was found, to attack both the form and the layout as one. Outdated elements in the ornament were taken as evidence for incompetent planning, and vice versa.

However, we are here concerned only with the ornament and it is important to understand what formed Owen's view, as well as the extent to which he controlled the designs. Owen is castigated for his upper-class connections in contrast to Huxley as the champion of popular science. Yet one should not underestimate the struggles that Owen had in building his career, from his time as Curator of the Hunterian Museum to the point at which he was able to sit in his new office as Superintendent of The Natural History Museum, eventually to retire at the end of a long day to his grace-and-favour home in Sheen Lodge. In order to achieve his goal of a specialist museum, he would have been forced to court the influential and the wealthy, since, on his appointment to the Natural History Department of the British Museum, there was not a single scientist among the Trustees. His concept of a new museum on an out of town site was a bold move, for which he needed the support of the great and the good. The sort of opposition he had to face was epitomised by WH Gregory, MP, who complained that he 'did not wish to see all the institutions of the country fall into the grasp of that craving, meddling, flattering, toadying, self-seeking clique that had established itself at Kensington'.[13] Yet it is significant that it was the evolutionists, the followers of Darwin and Huxley and champions of a populist science, who argued for the dispersal of the British Museum collections, pressing for just the move Owen achieved.

56   That Owen appears to have made a deliberate effort to cultivate major figures of the establishment is hardly surprising, given that his career as a naturalist began as early as 1832, with his *Memoir on the Pearly Nautilus*,[14] when science was still regarded as the leisured avocation of a gentleman rather than as the paid employment of a professional. At that period, most of the leading naturalists were themselves part of the establishment as clerics in the Church of England, or aristocrats with the means to indulge their interest. This is not to belittle the quality or range of scientific enquiry of the period; the advances were considerable. However, it serves to explain Owen's readiness to link himself to that particular milieu. Nicholas Rupke has traced Owen's connections with William Buckland, the naturalist Dean of Westminster;[15] which would help to explain the Christian iconography in his Museum. The creationist imagery of the façade was, not surprisingly, crowned by a terracotta statue of Adam. James Bell, wrote of the figure enthusiastically in the *Magazine of Art*:

> "glancing upward over the whole field of its varied and orderly scheme of enrichment, the eye rests upon the consummation of the whole in the figure which terminates appropriately the highest gable. There standing erect is seen the quintessence of nature, with outstretched arms and upward gaze directed towards a still higher power."[16]

Such a Christian view of the hierarchy of the species would have been no more than conventional in 1880, in spite of the growing acceptance of evolution, and it is simplistic to label Owen a creationist, without qualification. Although Huxley attacked his thesis as one that might 'be read backwards, or forwards or sideways, with exactly the same amount of signification',[17] Owen had long accepted some sort of migration of species. By 1862, he was speaking of an 'ordained continuous becoming of organic forms', which he considered was entirely within the workings of Divine Providence. His was, therefore, not a completely static universe, although an absolute distinction was encapsulated in the plan he had drawn for the future Museum – a view of the natural world that was outdated by the time the Museum was opened.

The key figure in this advance was, of course, Darwin, whom Huxley championed so vigorously. Darwin died in 1882 and was heroised with burial in Westminster Abbey, celebrating, as it were, 'the vast, unfinished social transformation that England was undergoing'.[18] The enormous impact of his theory of evolution was recognised by the installation, in 1885, of his statue at the focal point of Owen's Index Museum, where Waterhouse's great flight of stairs reaches its first landing. It might have been something of a blow to Owen, recently retired, to see pride of place in his Museum taken by a naturalist whose views were regarded as demolishing his. There is even a sketch in Waterhouse's hand for redesigning the terracotta to frame the statue.[19] But the alterations were never carried out and there is a certain justice in the fact that it is now Owen's statue that stares down fiercely from poll position while Darwin is removed to sit beside Huxley in the former Museum of British Natural History.

Yet the divide between Darwin and Owen may have been less dramatic than Huxley wished it to be. Darwin's nervous approach to Owen, and Owen's reluctance to be manoeuvred into an open clash with the most influential naturalist in the land, are well documented. They knew each other well enough; it had been Owen, as we have seen, who oversaw the eventual publication of *Zoology of the Voyage of HMS Beagle*. We have also noted that this contact may have had an echo in the ornamental roundel of the rhea. Waterhouse's incorporation of monkeys on the soaring arches of the Index Museum must surely be taken as an acknowledgement of Darwinian theories (fig 55). And it should be remembered that one of the missing sketches, for the lunette over the doorways at the ends of the west galleries, was of monkeys, matching the dodo in the east galleries. What is not clear, is whether this was ordered by Owen, or suggested by Waterhouse.

In the context of the narrow circle of Victorian scientific and professional men, it becomes relevant to explore some wider connections. Much of this exploration has to be speculative, but the personalities and their experiences are clear enough. The potential links are there. Darwin and Owen, we know, were well acquainted. So, too, were Waterhouse and Owen, even if only at the level of architect and client. However, it is also possible that Waterhouse had contact with Darwin's personal circle. Despite Darwin's well-known reclusiveness, it is even possible that they met; but it is certain that they had close acquaintances in common, and thus Darwin and his ideas will in all likelihood have been known to Waterhouse, if only at second hand. He could very well have had access to a more advanced view of the natural world than Owen had suggested for his walls; and there is every reason to believe that his free-thinking Quaker background would have rendered him open to such ideas. At any rate, the potential connection is worth recording. In 1880, Horace Darwin, Charles' youngest son, married Ida Farrer, for whose father Waterhouse had designed Abinger Hall in Surrey at precisely the time he was working on the Museum. It is known that Darwin visited Abinger Hall, but there are also strong links between Thomas Henry Farrer and Waterhouse, who may have been a regular visitor there during and shortly after construction. Farrer was a barrister of Lincoln's Inn and Waterhouse had many legal connections, not least his brother Theodore, who also trained at Lincoln's Inn. Farrer, who was precisely the same age as Waterhouse, had been educated at Eton, to which Waterhouse was at the time sending his son Paul, and Balliol, where Paul would go in 1880, and where Waterhouse himself was busy designing extensive new buildings. Waterhouse will certainly have met Farrer as a client, but it is more than likely that, with such closely overlapping connections, they could have developed a closer relationship.

Mrs Waterhouse regularly gave dinner parties – 'Mrs Waterhouse's dim delicious Thursdays'[20] as one guest described them and gathered a broadly based intellectual circle including guests from the world of art and architecture. Benjamin Jowett, the dynamic Master of Balliol College, was one regular visitor, and his open-minded scholarship may well have led conversation into topical fields such as evolution. It was he, after all, who had suggested in *Essays and Reviews* (1860), a publication that was quite as much a *succès de scandale* as *On the Origin of Species*, that the Bible should be the subject of textual criticism just like any other ancient manuscript. It was all part of the new scholarship, and one can easily imagine lively discussion in the elegant drawing room of 20 (now 67) New Cavendish Street. And it is not entirely speculative to suggest that Waterhouse may have had some interest in questions of natural history and evolution. Another of his close friends, and a regular guest, was the young author Edmund Gosse, whose father was an eminent zoologist and fundamentalist Christian.[21] The subject must often have arisen.

There are further possible connections to be explored. Owen, it is well known, had links with the circle of scholars centred on Christ Church in Oxford. It is sometimes suggested that this may have played a part in distancing him from the Darwin camp, which was rooted in Cambridge. However, it is probably more relevant that it brought him into contact with Dr Henry Acland, the moving force

behind the Oxford University Museum. This building was one of relatively few precedents for the sort of scientific museum Owen was planning; it was also one of the principal architectural talking points of the 1860s. Waterhouse was undoubtedly aware of the work, and may very well have visited it when he was in Oxford superintending work at Balliol. He had, in any case, already had some contact with Sir Thomas Deane, the senior partner of the Oxford Museum's designer Benjamin Woodward, in one of his early commissions.[22] He undoubtedly knew about the illustrative sculptural decoration there, for he was himself employing the O'Shea brothers, who were responsible for the ornamental carving.[23] He had probably scrutinised the series of finely carved capitals with portraits of plants that were gradually being completed there, and it is highly likely that the building influenced both Waterhouse and Owen. Its geological didacticism finds a small echo at The Natural History Museum in the provision of twenty window-sills in the former Refreshment Room of different polished building stones. I suspect, however, that Waterhouse felt the plastic approach to sculpture that was required for terracotta would give him greater control, as well as being easier to alter and, therefore, cheaper. It was also, as we have seen, integral to the construction, and thus could not be left unfinished.

The geological element at South Kensington, the only one of its kind in the Museum's decoration, is a reminder that there were other professionals involved in the Museum. The departmental keepers will have had their own views, and there is a good deal of correspondence in the Museum archives between these senior staff and Waterhouse, mostly about the arrangement of their departments and the design of appropriate display cases. However, that does not preclude their giving him some advice on the sorts of creatures he might include in the decoration. Waterhouse was already known to Antony Panizzi, the dynamic, though recently retired, Librarian of the British Museum, since his work at Balliol involved alterations to Panizzi's house there. The correspondence files show that he also dealt frequently with Panizzi's successors, John Winter Jones and Edward Augustus Bond. Any of these three could have helped point him to useful visual sources in the Museum's library.

A hint that the librarians were involved comes in a letter from Waterhouse to John Winter Jones. After commenting that the ornament was intended 'to represent, on one side,

56. Detail of the ceiling panels of the Entrance Hall, the plant in the middle is identified as *Nicotiana tabacum*.

58 various forms of extinct life, and on the other, various forms of existing life', he continued:

"May I ask if you think the Trustees would at all incline to place one of the Professors in communication with me to whom I might show the models of the various illustrations proposed and who would thus prevent the possible commission of what might be regarded as serious scientific errors."[24]

A few weeks later, the minutes record that Owen had 'conferred with the architect on the subject of the proposed ornamentation of the New Museum; and has furnished him with figures and outlines of upwards of fifty restorations of extinct animals for that purpose'.[25] This is more specific than the 'numerous figures' referred to in his son's biography, and suggests that Owen probably advised on the extinct creatures rather than on all classes of life. In that case, Waterhouse may well have turned to other departmental keepers, or sketched actual specimens in the various departments at the British Museum. He certainly got to know most of the departmental keepers and occasional contact with a range of such staff could explain the slightly random way in which groups of models are identified with scientific names or left undescribed. Two names occur frequently in the correspondence. George Robert Waterhouse, apparently no relation, was Keeper of Geology from 1857–1880 and wrote regularly to Alfred Waterhouse about a range of details. He may well have helped him with the depiction of fossils such as those on the basement window mullions or in the capitals of the east galleries. It might also have been he who provided the illustrations of extinct varieties of fish that allowed Waterhouse such a long list of species for the bases of his piers. However, many of the objects in GR Waterhouse's collection were not particularly suited for inclusion in the ornamental scheme. Another keeper whose concerns were frequently conveyed to Waterhouse was William Carruthers, Keeper of Botany from 1871 to 1895. No correspondence survives about the ornamental versions of plants, though his name occurs in a number of notes on the drawings. However, he arrived at the Museum at almost the same time as Waterhouse began work on the structure and though it might be merely a coincidence that the botanical ornaments of the ceilings are so completely identified, it is certainly tempting to believe that Waterhouse talked to Carruthers about the plants, and even discussed the selection of species with him (fig 56).

In the light of this long speculative quest, we may reconsider the relative parts played by Waterhouse and Owen in designing the Museum. What seems clear is that no one scientist was responsible for the entire selection of species. It is more likely that Waterhouse was given a range of suggestions to choose from once Owen's overall division had been decided. The keepers, too, were naturally more concerned with the disposition of their departments and arrangements for display or movement of specimens. If Waterhouse was given freedom within the overall constraint of the division between east and west wings, that would account for the extent to which his depictions of species need to be regarded as generic rather than specific or scientifically accurate portrayals. And there are hints in the drawings that he was prepared to be a little cavalier with Owen's distinction between living and extinct species: for instance, in the way the iron silhouettes of the roof cresting (plates 48 & 49) are used freely on both wings, with the honourable exception of the pterodactyl, which appears only on the east.

Another factor that needs to be acknowledged is the weakness of the ornamental scheme as a complete summary of natural history. There are considerable gaps in the coverage. The exigencies of space presumably account for the lack of whales or any of the larger mammals, such as giraffes or elephants. There are no crocodiles and only a couple of snakes, while the vast and popular enterprise of butterfly and beetle collecting are acknowledged in a selection of little more than half a dozen examples (fig 57).

57. Beetle roundel in the mullion of a basement window of the west wing.

58. Air-brick in the basement in the form of a spider in its web.

Even the spider and her web only squeeze in under the guise of an air-brick (fig 58). Another particularly interesting gap in the ornament is the absence of dinosaurs, apart from the notable exceptions already cited. Here again, the problem of scale made it virtually impossible to include any of the larger animals among the plethora of smaller-scale creatures, but their absence is the more surprising when we remember that it was precisely at this period that the first reconstructions of dinosaurs were being made. Their identification had been very much part of Owen's interest with his major work, published as *The History of British Fossil Mammals and Birds* in 1846, and his description of the archaeopterix in 1863. He was also one of the jurors for the Great Exhibition, with the task of overseeing the construction of a series of full-size dinosaur replicas that still adorn an island in Crystal Palace Park (figs 59 & 60). The absence of these creatures would be the more surprising if he had been directly selecting species for the decoration.

The Great Exhibition models were well publicised at the time; a dinner was famously held in the iguanodon, pictured in the *Illustrated London News*.[26] Indeed, such was the interest in these monsters, that even the sculptor's workshop was illustrated. They are especially important because they reveal the concern for detail and accuracy that Owen applied to the supervision of their creation:

"Those extinct animals were first selected of which the entire, or nearly entire skeleton had been examined in a

fossil state. To accurate drawings of these skeletons an outline of the form of the entire animal was added, according to the properties and relations of the skin and adjacent soft parts to the superficial parts of the skeleton… From such an outline of the exterior, Mr Waterhouse Hawkins prepared at once a miniature model in clay. This model was rigorously tested in regard to all its proportions with those exhibited by the bones and joints of the skeleton of the fossil animal and the required alterations and modifications were successively made after repeated examinations and comparisons, until the results proved satisfactory. The next step was to make a copy merely of the proof model of the natural size of the extinct animal."[27]

The final stage was the casting of the whole in cement.. The modelling process is important here because it was in many ways similar to that employed for making the terracotta. If Owen was so closely involved in the creation of these spectacular monsters, one might wonder why he was apparently less involved in the decoration of his Museum. Of course, replicas of actual dinosaurs were of a different order from architectural decoration and it is significant that Waterhouse had been very careful to ensure he had Owen's approval before going ahead with his model making. On 12 October 1874 he wrote to Owen:

"I should feel greatly obliged if you would take some early opportunity of calling at our works at South Kensington & looking at some models which Dujardin has

59. Crystal Palace Park, Sydenham, dinosaur made by Benjamin Waterhouse Hawkins in 1854.

60   prepared of extinct creatures. Until you have seen them I hardly like to perpetuate them in Terra Cotta."[28]

Only six of the dated drawings are from 1874, and of these, two are for abstract designs and one for plants. The remaining three (plates 1–3), all dated November,[29] may possibly be among those that Owen was invited to inspect. What makes Waterhouse's nervousness more understandable is that one was for the monkeys of the great entrance arches. Given the evolution controversy, and that Owen had worked on chimpanzees and apes, Waterhouse may well have wished to have his monkeys checked before they were sent for manufacture. On the other hand, since the menagerie included such creatures as the palaeotherium, which Owen had also described, it is unfortunate that we have no evidence whether or not he actually looked at that model before it was sent for manufacture. The picture is tantalisingly vague, and one has the distinct impression that by the mid-1870s, when the ornamental modelling was well underway, Owen had satisfied himself that he had a sound architect and a good modeller and was prepared to let them get on with the task on their own. As Nicholas Rupke has shown, Owen was more interested in museum politics than in scientific politics and one might suppose that he had more pressing matters to concern himself with than the details of the ornament. Besides, it would have been a great deal easier for him, dropping in at Waterhouse's office, or even over dinner in New Cavendish Street, to look over a sheaf of sketches and suggest modifications there and then. The ornament could never be the sort of exact scientific replication that Owen or his colleagues would have accepted as actually illustrative of species. Terracotta, after all, cannot mimic the minute differences of texture and colour that are crucial to the distinction of species. The whole business of scientifically informed ornament was simply a triumphant example of that archetypically Victorian endeavour to marry Science and Art. We have to accept, from the lack of any suggestion of complaint, that Waterhouse succeeded in satisfying Owen whilst managing to modify the poses, scale and habitats of his clay creatures so that they would fit onto the building.

60. Crystal Palace Park, general view of the island with Benjamin Waterhouse Hawkins's dinosaurs, made in 1854.

Notes

1 The idea was developed and published three years later as a pamphlet 'On the Extent and Aims of a National Museum of Natural History', London, 1862.

2 The Rev R Owen, *The Life of Richard Owen*, 2 vols, John Murray, London, 1894.

3 See Jean M Ingles & Frederick C Sawyer, 'A catalogue of the Richard Owen collection of Palaeontological and Zoological drawings in the British Museum (Natural History)', in *Bulletin of the British Museum (Natural History)*, Historical Series, vol 6, no 5, 25 Oct 1979. It is not always clear at what date the drawings were acquired by Owen, but the vast majority could have been available by the time he was selecting images for Waterhouse.

4 See Carla Yanni, 'Divine Display or Secular Science: Defining Nature at the Natural History Museum in London', in *Journal of the Society of Architectural Historians*, vol 55, no 3, September 1996, fig 19, p292.

5 *Zoology of the Voyage of HMS Beagle under the command of Captain Fitzroy, RN, during the years 1832-1836*, 5 vols, Smith Elder, London, 1840–43.

6 The details of Owen's involvement at The Natural History Museum and the relationship between architecture and the natural sciences are extensively discussed by Yanni in *Construction of Nature in British Victorian Architecture & Architectural Theory*, University of Pennsylvania PhD thesis, 1994. Her ideas are further elaborated in 'Divine Display', op. cit. and, more recently in *Nature's Museums: Victorian Science & the Architecture of Display*, Athlone Press (London), 1999. I am very much indebted to her for letting me see drafts of her material, and have drawn extensively on her published work.

7 See Yanni, 'Divine Display', op. cit. p295.

8 *The Field*, 28 April 1881, quoted in WT Stearn, *The Natural History Museum at South Kensington*, Heinemann, London, 1981, p49.

9 PRO Work 17 16/2. Ms letter from AW to First Commissioner of Works, 4 May 1868.

10 Quoted in Yanni, PhD thesis, op. cit. p266.

11 Ibid p263-4, quoting *The Daily News*, 6 September 1879.

12 Yanni, *Nature's Museums*, op. cit. traces the evolution of the type and the divergent world views the various examples embodied.

13 Hansard, vol 171, 15 June 1863, cols 922–3.

14 He began in practice as a surgeon as early as 1826, setting up in Cook's Court, Carey Street, a building later redeveloped by Waterhouse. *The Memoir on the Pearly Nautilus* was his first scientific study, a detailed description of the hitherto imperfectly identified species.

15 Nicholas Rupke, *Richard Owen, Victorian Naturalist*, Yale University Press, New Haven, 1994.

16 Quoted in Yanni, PhD thesis, op. cit. p265.

17 Quoted in Adrian Desmond, *Huxley*, Penguin Books, Harmondsworth, 1998, p304.

18 Adrian Desmond & James Moore, *Darwin*, Penguin Books, Harmondsworth, 1992, p677.

19 RIBA Drawings Collection. Wat [56]. The scene of the dedication was pictured in *The Illustrated London News*, See Yanni, PhD thesis, op cit, fig 6.1.

20 The phrase is quoted in *The Centenary of Elizabeth Waterhouse, 1834–1934*, by LV Holdsworth, p8, (reprinted from *Friends' Quarterly Examiner*, July 1934). See also *Cunningham & Waterhouse 1992*, p105.

21 The story of Philip Henry Gosse's (1810–1888) obsessive maintaining of a creationist theology is told in Edmund Gosse's masterpiece, *Father and Son*, 1907.

22 See Colin Cunningham & Prudence Waterhouse, *Alfred Waterhouse 1830–1905: Biography of a Practice*, OUP, Oxford, 1992, p22.

23 Waterhouse commissioned the O'Shea brothers, along with Thomas Woolner and several others, to produce samples of carving for his Manchester Assize Courts in the early 1860s. He deemed the screen that they made for the hall of the Judge's Lodgings their finest work.

24 The Natural History Museum Archives, Minutes of the Standing Committee and Sub-Committee on Buildings and Natural History. Ms letter AW to J Winter Jones, 7 Nov 1873.

25 Natural History Museum, Archives. Minute Book of the Department of Natural History, 20 Nov 1873.

26 *Illustrated London News*, vol 12, 1854, illustrated as fig 22 in Yanni, 'Divine Display', op. cit.

27 Richard Owen, *Geology and Inhabitants of the ancient world described by R Owen: the animals constructed by B Hawkins*, Crystal Palace Library (London), 1854.

28 Alfred Waterhouse to Professor Richard Owen, 12 Oct 1874. The Natural History Museum Library & Archives, OC.

29 Two are for birds and foliage for the Index Museum, ground floor, and are noted 'Sent to Manufacturers 25th Nov 1874' and 'Sent to Manufacturers 20th Nov 1874'; the final drawing, for monkey arches in the Entrance Hall, is noted 'November 24th 1874' (Drawings vol I.1, 2 & 3).

V
the sculptor's contribution

61. Exterior view of the Museum, 1881. (H Dixon, The Natural History Museum Archives)

Architect and scientist were both clearly central to the whole scheme, but it would be impossible to understand the quality of the Museum's decoration, or, indeed, fully appreciate the pencil sketches, without some knowledge of how the designs were turned into three-dimensional models, and by whom. Waterhouse had a reputation for meticulousness that would never allow him to accept substandard workmanship. He once halted work on a bank he was building in the City because the ornamental carvers were not operating to his satisfaction, and were putting too much detail into Gothic beasts intended only to be viewed

62. One of the earliest examples of the terracotta revival in Britain – texts surrounding the main door of Edmund Sharpe's Church of St Stephen Lever Bridge, Lancs, of 1842-5.

63

from thirty-five feet below. At the Museum, a major public building on an important site in the capital city, the architect, who had relatively recently arrived from the provinces, would have been determined to accept only the best.

It had been a bold decision in 1870 to face the whole of the Museum in terracotta (fig 61). The Museum was the first large building to be clad entirely in what was still a relatively new material, and there were to be difficulties in finding the skilled labour to build the plain walls, let alone the ornamental pieces. It was as well that the architect was Waterhouse, a thoroughly professional man with an eye for detail. As early as 1871 he had written to the First Commissioner of Works, 'In preparing the specification of the work it is necessary to consider with especial care that part of it which relates to the Terra Cotta',[1] warning that 'there are, in this country, not more than four or five firms who manufacture what may be called really satisfactory Terra Cotta'.[2] He urged getting estimates from several of the best manufacturers and 'as a preliminary step [begged] to apply for permission to get models prepared for certain portions of the work: such models to be cast in plaster and duplicates sent to each Terra Cotta maker invited to tender'.[3]

This was before the designs were drawn for any of the ornament, before even the basic building contract had been let, but it was precisely the sort of attention to detail that would ensure the successful completion of the ornament. However, we have already seen that one of the surprising facts about Waterhouse's sketches is that, although they are designs for three-dimensional terracotta, often in high relief, almost all are drawn from one viewpoint only, when one might have expected him to produce more than one elevation, plans and even sections. Only three drawings (plates 33–34 & 67) show a creature from more than one viewpoint and it would seem that the craftsman must have had a good deal of freedom. This implies that Waterhouse found one on whom he was happy to rely.

The complex relationship between Waterhouse and the number of different people who made his creatures was crucial. At the end of the line was the builder, George Baker, who had to set the finished pieces on the building. His problems included the need to receive and store the thousands of different terracotta blocks, ornamental and plain, in such a way that they would not be damaged and would be readily available when needed. Packed in their straw-filled crates, the blocks would have been difficult to distinguish, whereas, once unpacked, they would be at risk of being chipped and rendered useless. This is very different from traditional construction with brick and stone ornament and one can readily imagine the potential for chaos and loss of time as Baker attempted to keep track of individual pieces on a busy building site, and to balance the record of the orders placed by the Clerk of Works against the manufacturers' delivery notes.

But these were minor problems, and Waterhouse's care in designing each block ensured, at least, that there was no difficulty over fitting. This was crucial, since a terracotta block, once fired, cannot be shaved down or altered on site to make it fit in the way a block of stone may be. The precision was partly ensured by those penultimate in the line, the actual manufacturers, Messrs Gibbs and Canning of Tamworth. Waterhouse worked with a number of terracotta manufacturers in the course of his career and had just placed a large order with this particular company in their hands for internal facing in Manchester Town Hall; he may have been relieved that the Office of Works was prepared to accept a tender from a company with whom he was already familiar. In spite of the occasional failure, they proved reliable suppliers. Yet there was the prior problem of making the models from which the moulds could be taken. Most manufacturers had their own modelling shop, where workmen would make clay models from shrinkage-scale drawings. These in turn would be cased in plaster to make moulds from which the blocks would be cast.

63. Aston Webb and Ingress Bell made spectacular use of terracotta for the exterior of the Birmingham Assize Courts in 1887–91.

Waterhouse was not prepared to leave this to anonymous workmen in a distant factory. Modelling was the key to the whole process, which required a competent craftsman whose work Waterhouse could supervise more easily than by visiting the factory. He needed someone on hand in London who could be relied upon to interpret his sketches faithfully and who had a real understanding of his aims and the qualities required for his ornament. Such a person would not be easy to find.

The enigmatic M Dujardin was evidently a new type of craftsman, the sculptor-modeller, whose skill was in turning other people's designs into three-dimensional models for casting. There was no real craft tradition upon which such people could draw, since the use of terracotta had hitherto been largely confined to modelling relatively straightforward ornament on simple blocks (fig 62). It was not until the end of the century that it became common for entire surfaces to be treated plastically (fig 63). By the time the Museum had been open a decade, terracotta had become a regular feature of the ordered ornament that clad steel framed buildings in both Britain and America, as well as being a means of adding great richness where required (figs 64 & 65). Waterhouse had been both a pioneer and a leading practitioner. He developed an extensive language of modelled ornament for his exteriors, and for the interiors that he regularly clad with moulded and glazed faience (figs 66–68). He had learned to use the material in almost any stylistic mode – Classical or Gothic – and designed whole buildings, large and small, in the material, using its visual potential to the full (figs 69 & 70). Yet The Natural History Museum was his first and greatest endeavour in the medium.

65. A richly ornamented doorway in the churrigueresque style adorns the Million Dollar Theatre in Los Angeles of 1918.

64. Terracotta panels beneath the windows of the Wainwright Building, St Louis Mo, by Louis Sullivan, 1890–1.

66. A series of simple floral bands and moulded sections make a richly-corbelled corner oriel for the Prudential Building in Liverpool of 1886.

66

The ornamental language he developed there is unique and daring, requiring the support of a highly-skilled team to bring it to fruition.

At the very start of the commission, Waterhouse had persuaded the government to allow him to have sample models made. This was done by three different firms or craftsmen: Bunnett & Co, Hodkinson & Co and a Mr BJ Morris.[4] Since their names do not recur in relation to the Museum, it may be that they did not show the promise he hoped for. Another leading carver, JW Seale, had already proved unsatisfactory at the bank Waterhouse had built in Lombard Street and he may well have been concerned as to the best way forward. He turned to the rising firm of Farmer & Brindley, who had already done a good deal of work for Scott. William Brindley himself was just finishing the stone ornament of the Albert Memorial, so Waterhouse could have inspected his work easily. With that sort of recommendation, and the fact that their Works was conveniently situated in Westminster Bridge Road, Waterhouse probably felt he could rely on them. They were certainly the sort of firm that was used to working with freedom, for, as Emma Hardy has pointed out, Scott never made detailed drawings for the ornament of his buildings.[5] They had already done some small amounts of work for Waterhouse and were soon to become his favourite ornamental carvers, working on upwards of 100 commissions for him. He quickly established a good relationship with them and was able to rest easy in the knowledge that they would see that his drawings were properly interpreted.

In the early 1870s, William Farmer and his partner William Brindley were trading as sculptors, but were exclusively engaged in providing what was known as 'architectural sculpture': repetitive carved ornament of all sorts, made to order for buildings. What was unusual about the present contract was that Waterhouse employed them only to make models for his terracotta ornament. So well satisfied was he with their work that he continued this practice until the end of his career. However, in 1870 their partnership was newly formed, and was only just beginning the process of expansion that made Messrs Farmer & Brindley one of the leading producers of architectural sculpture and ornament. Farmer had been in business as a stonemason since at least 1860, though by 1865 he was describing himself as a sculptor. Brindley did not become a partner until about 1870,[6] when the firm was obviously growing fast.

It was apparently in this new phase of their enterprise that the firm took on the young Frenchman, Dujardin, allocating him to The Natural History Museum job. The achievement of the ornamental scheme is generally seen as the triumphant collaboration between Waterhouse and Dujardin, yet the sculptor remains a shadowy figure. So little is known about him that we cannot even be sure of his initial; it appears the M stands for no more than Monsieur. It has been suggested that he was the Auguste Dujardin who exhibited a marble relief medallion at the 1866 Salon.[7] If so, he was only about twenty-five when he was given the job of making models for Waterhouse. One wonders why a young sculptor such as he would have come to London. Perhaps he had relatives whom he felt might help him launch a career. Certainly there was a Louis Dujardin in business as a cabinet-maker in Clerkenwell in the 1860s and 1870s,[8] but his address in Somers Town does not suggest either affluence or potential influence. It is possible that Waterhouse had met the young man in Paris and encouraged him to come over.[9] That would have been in keeping with his encouragement of the young sculptor Hamo Thornycroft, whom he helped to a commission at Eaton Hall at this time. If Waterhouse did know Dujardin, he would certainly have been in a position to get him employment with Messrs Farmer & Brindley. Whatever the details of his relationship with them, Dujardin makes only this fleeting appearance on the British scene. Perhaps he did not stay long in England. By 1881, at all events, he was no longer resident in London. He might have returned to Paris, or equally possibly, he could have crossed the Atlantic to work as a modeller in the burgeoning terracotta industry of America.[10] Maybe he was disappointed with the status his employment with Farmer & Brindley brought; there is certainly a hint that he did not get the credit he hoped for with his work at The Natural History Museum. *The Building News*, presumably repeating briefing notes from the architect, recorded that 'the decorative details were modelled by Mr Du Jardin'.[11] Their report was followed by a sharp riposte from Farmer & Brindley:

"Sir, In your descriptive report of these (Natural History Museum) works in your last week's number you state 'the decorative details were modelled by Mr Du Jardin'. It should be by Messrs. Farmer & Brindley, their foreman being Mr Du Jardin."[12]

This ungenerous note led to an even sharper rebuke from a correspondent who was almost certainly John Ruskin. The writer asks Farmer & Brindley to say 'who did model these charming details if Mr Dujardin did not' and, before signing himself 'JR', wonders whether Farmer & Brindley may not be a little jealous.[13] What was important, however, was the recognition that the modeller did have an important role.

The terracotta creations that resulted are nothing if not charming. Though they faithfully reproduce Waterhouse's sketch designs, they owe a good deal of their character to their modeller. In the case of the great beasts on the cornice, for example, Dujardin must have had considerable freedom. Given that there is only the one drawing, no side elevations or even plans to show how they would fit on their bases, the overall dimensions and the size of the base itself must have been sufficient for both architect and modeller. Waterhouse only provided four vigorous profiles and two full-frontal views. His decision to allow the craftsman to work freely, producing according to his own skill within an overall instruction as to size and shape fitted precisely with the aims of the Gothic revival. It would have been just the sort of thing to appeal to Ruskin, who was still the doyen of architectural taste. Yet that approach would hardly have required the detailed drawings that Waterhouse produced (fig 3, p11); and we have to recognise that, although the 'truth to nature' of his drawings was fully in accord with fashionable Ruskinian doctrines, Waterhouse was not going about things entirely as the master would have approved. The reason is twofold. First, it is likely that he was conscious of the example of the University Museum at Oxford, with which Ruskin had been personally involved. This was probably the most celebrated scientific museum building of the mid-century, and was barely a dozen years old when Waterhouse began work at South Kensington.[14] Like Waterhouse's structure, it had been designed to be decorated with images of plants and animals. In fact, the the Irish craftsman James O'Shea was famously sacked following his carving of Darwinian monkeys around the entrance arch. But the building was designed on strictly Gothic lines, with the images to be carved in stone, and when Waterhouse was designing, the carving at Oxford was still unfinished; the interior capitals were not completed until 1912 and the exterior remains only partly carved to this day. Waterhouse was determined that his building would not suffer the same sad fate as the Oxford Museum, even if the government, who were paying, were determined to keep costs to a minimum. He therefore chose terracotta, which had to be ornamented before it was fixed on the building. Stone was regularly carved after building, and nothing would have been easier than to withhold funds for carving once the structure was finished. With terracotta, completion of the structure and completion of the ornament would be one and the same thing. In choosing terracotta and drawing the ornament himself, Waterhouse was proving himself more than simply a disciple of Ruskin. He and his client had chosen merely to start from the Ruskinian principal of deriving ornament from nature, applying it scientifically to the practical processes of building.

Terracotta was not an entirely new material for Waterhouse, but it required careful handling. The material's nature, and its very modernity, were further reasons for abandoning Ruskinian principles. The Natural History Museum was probably the first major building in the world to be fully-faced externally and internally with this material and Waterhouse had never used it so extensively before. He was trying it at just this moment in Manchester Town Hall, but only as an interior fire-proof facing. Much earlier in his career he had even advised against its use in restoring Rydal church in the Lake District. Now he was launched on a major project using a material that still almost constituted an experiment for him, and one that made immense demands on both architect and builder. In those circumstances, it is understandable that he wanted to remain fully in control of the process.

The drawings he produced demonstrate that he made himself personally responsible for each item, and the modelled results are surprisingly close to his sketches. The mechanical process of casting did, on several occasions, lead to his sketches being reversed (compare figs 91 & 92 with plates 13 & 89), but this does not seem to have bothered him at all. However, the act of turning Waterhouse's two-dimensional sketches into the rich relief that forms the actual decoration required a high degree of skill. There is evidence that Dujardin was involved in more than just the floral and animal work. Three of the surviving constructional drawings bear notes requiring details to be 'modelled by Dujardin', (fig 8, p16) in one case 'for Mr Waterhouse to see'.[15] These refer to such items as the VR monograms on the undersides of the gallery beams, along with finials for the second floor, suggesting that Dujardin may even have been trusted to work from the smaller-scale architectural drawings. The whole system of working meant that Waterhouse relied entirely on his sculptor to judge the appropriate depth of relief and the delicacy or

67. A window of the Refuge Assurance Building in Manchester, designed by Waterhouse in 1891.

68. Waterhouse regularly linked exterior terracotta with glazed faience for the interior, as here at Foster's Bank, Cambridge, 1891. The Natural History Museum is unique, however, in using only terracotta both internally and externally.

69. Interior of the Parrot House at Eaton Hall, designed by Waterhouse in 1880.

70. The Parrot House at Eaton Hall, dating from 1880, is a rare excursus into the Classical style by Waterhouse, executed entirely in golden terracotta.

vigour of the modelling. Recent experience of replacing some of the larger beasts for restoration gives an indication of the sculptural task involved in creating them in the first place (fig 71). Waterhouse was very fortunate to find a craftsman on whom he could depend so fully, and it is both sad and frustrating that Dujardin remains relatively anonymous. We do not even know the limits of his involvement at The Natural History Museum. It seems unlikely, for instance, that he would have been involved with the cut-metal creatures of the ridge cresting (plates 48 & 49), and we can only wonder whether it was he who produced the model for the set of six cast-iron lions who sit in their gilding on the gate piers (fig 21).

It is hardly surprising, although unfortunate, that not a single autograph model from Dujardin's hand survives. This makes it extremely difficult to assess the precise nature of his contribution, and by extension, the real purpose of the drawings. Given the tantalising claim in Farmer & Brindley's letter that he was their 'foreman', it must certainly be wondered whether Dujardin actually modelled all the creatures himself, or even that he executed the majority. His is the only name we know, but the sheer number of models – more than 475 separate pieces from the surviving sketches alone – would have been an extraordinary achievement for one sculptor working over a mere four years. The feat is probably not impossible, but it is at least

71. A lion for the parapet being modelled in clay in preparation for making the mould and casting a replacement. The damaged original is to the left. (Photo courtesy of Ibstock Hathernware Ltd)

likely that some of the other anonymous craftsmen employed by Farmer & Brindley played a part. The patterned shafts of the entrance doorway, for instance (fig 79) would not necessarily have required the sole attention of the foreman, nor would such things as the florets from the soffit of the great monkey arches, despite the fact they are made in a variety of different forms (fig 72). It is most likely, therefore, that junior modellers worked alongside Dujardin from Waterhouse's drawings. Quite possibly, such men were allowed to work independently on smaller items such as the starfish and other sea creatures for the basement windows. Maybe a reliable workman would have been left alone to model something such as the air-bricks of the basement (fig 73). Equally, it may have fallen to assistants to work on the more repetitive patterns of foliage that connected the rows of birds and monkeys on the great arches. It is impossible to know where the division of labour came, and it may even be true that Dujardin was, as Farmer & Brindley claimed, no more than their foreman, responsible for quality control rather than for creating the sculptures himself.

There is a further, more menial, but important role to consider. The models sent to the terracotta manufacturers

72. Section of simple foliage ornament
for the soffit of the monkey arches
(see vol I no 45).

73. Air-brick in the basement in the form of
an extinct marine creature in a net pattern.

had to be in the form of exact replicas of the various blocks to be manufactured, rather than merely of the creatures that perched on them. For the manufacture of simple blocks, an exact profile drawing was all that was needed, and the clay could be extruded by machine. For the ornament, however, this was not enough: a plaster model had to be made. This required careful building-up without too much undercutting, otherwise it would be impossible to make the mould. The blocks also had to take account of the way in which they would course with the plain walling around. Waterhouse's sketches clearly take this into account. The monkeys, for instance (plates 3 & 4) were all designed to be on two blocks of different sizes, and great attention was paid to the way in which the join at their waists is pointed in the construction. With this system of manufacture, a modeller had to build up each of the mouldings and ribs on which Waterhouse relied so precisely for his architectural effects, as well as the creatures themselves. Just as the drawings were set up for Waterhouse by staff in his office, it is most likely that the more mechanical

building-up was done for Dujardin by others. One has to think of him as a member – though undoubtedly the leading member – of a team.

Whatever his abilities and scope, it must also have been the case that Dujardin understood the qualities of clay and was thoroughly versed in the business of plastic sculpture. If he had any academic or *atelier* training as a sculptor, it could have been assumed that he was thoroughly familiar with the processes of building up a model preparatory to casting. Yet, in exploring the craft relationship of architect and modeller, it is easy to forget what constraints the material and its manufacturing process themselves place on their users. Given that a terracotta block cannot be cut or shaved to fit precisely once it has been fired, every block and ornamental panel for the Museum had to be designed to a very precise tolerance so that when delivered it could simply be lifted into place and would fit exactly.[17] If that were not enough, as already noted, the designer had to compensate for the fact that clay shrinks (usually about one inch in every foot) in drying and firing. This was where Dujardin's skill came in, for he was able to take the delicate sketches Waterhouse produced and turn each into a fully-rounded original, roughly one twelfth over-size. It was the sort of thing that was regularly done in the modelling shops of terracotta manufacturers, where originals were painstakingly crafted for the mould makers (fig 74). We have no way of knowing whether Dujardin had worked in the terracotta industry before, but it was his responsibility to see that the artists designs were faithfully reproduced. He also had to ensure that the models were made in such a way that

72

74. A view of a typical terracotta modelling shop: in this case that of the New York Architectural Terra Cotta Co, c1900. (Photo courtesy of Friends of Terra Cotta Archives)

75. A mould for a baluster, with a finished baluster from the mould beside it, probably by Shaws of Darwen. (Photo courtesy of the Michael Stratton Archive)

76. Finished terracotta cornice blocks, for an unidentified building, about to leave the works – probably Shaws of Darwen. In the background are more blocks, packed with straw, ready for transport. (Photo courtesy of the Michael Stratton Archive)

77. Heavy-duty pug-mill, designed to extrude simple terracotta blocks, probably at the works of Shaws of Darwen. One block is partly visible to the left. (Photo courtesy of the Michael Stratton Archive)

What was required was a thorough understanding of the material and its processes of manufacture before either the builder or the designer could count on success. That is exactly what Mr Terra Cotta had. He understood how the material was manufactured, and how to design accordingly. He knew, for instance, that it would be impossible to cast really large blocks, so the animals of the cornice are designed to be made in two sections, the joins carefully concealed beneath their manes. He was well aware of the characteristics of different clays, and the fact that different clays and different kiln temperatures produced different colours, different hardnesses as well as different shrinkage. He almost certainly visited the manufacturer's workshops, where he would have seen how the models were cased in plaster of Paris to make moulds. Above all, he was fully aware that he was using a process of factory production, not individual crafting (fig 77). Waterhouse's understanding of the process and his careful choice of contractors ensured a particularly fine product. Through more than a century of wear and tear, including bomb damage, the terracotta on the Museum has held up remarkably well. A few blocks failed as the result of normal settlement, but the worst damage appears to have been the result of inappropriate cleaning.[18] Recent restoration has included replacement of the most seriously weakened blocks, including some of the beasts on the parapet. These have even included a 'mythical' alternative to the wolf on the west wing. This design is only loosely based on Waterhouse's sketch and stands out sharply because its head is turned the opposite way to the remaining originals (compare fig 78, and plate 35).

they could be easily used to make the mould. Once safely in the hands of Gibbs and Canning, the precious model was encased in plaster of Paris. The plaster casing was then cut into sections that could be reassembled and held with straps, leaving a void into which liquid clay could be poured to make the final block (fig 75). Once the clay had hardened, the pieces of the mould were removed and could be re-used, while the moulded clay block was allowed to dry, fired in a kiln and then shipped back to the construction site (fig 76).

The penalties for getting any of this wrong were considerable. The process took eight to ten weeks from finished model to delivery of the final block, and any replacement would therefore hold up the works. Just such a mishap did occur when one whole course of plain terracotta blocks came from the kiln in a defective state and had to be thrown away. Waterhouse was able to explain that stoppage to the Office of Works, but with over 150 different types of ornamental blocks for the front façade alone, it is not surprising he found the task complex. His problem appears even more daunting when one counts what was required for even a single bay of the wings. The total is 72 different types of ornamental block in various multiples amounting to 304 pieces in all! In the end, the difficulty of sorting, storing and fitting all those different blocks was too much for the builder, Baker, who eventually went bankrupt.

Modelling the individual blocks was clearly a job for a sculptor; but the use of plaster moulds could result in the finest of models being reproduced a number of times. However, the most sensible use of what was in effect a mechanical process was in the repetition of shapes. Thus Waterhouse's designs, for all their variety, rest on the rhythms created by the multiplication of images, not on

74 their unique character. The 150 different pieces of ornament on the façade turned into several thousand separate blocks. And the 134 designs in the Museum's Collection likewise appear many times over on the building. Generally speaking, the most carefully naturalistic depictions are designed as relief panels. The dodo lunette, (plate 127) for instance, or the four roundels of the Index Museum galleries (plates 80, 81, 98, 99 & 127) could thus be made in large slabs where there was less risk of distortion or an awkward joint that would spoil the image. However, Waterhouse used such items sparingly. The dodo panel was repeated only once, and the roundels are unique. Of the fourteen different panels for the great staircase, only two – the hare and the cavy (plates 91 & 93) – occur more than once. Such things were evidently intended to be the highlights in an overall scheme of enrichment that relied on repetition.

Michael Stratton has estimated that a plaster mould would allow about fifty castings before it became pock-marked and useless.[19] Although some of the minor elements at The Natural History Museum exceed that (and presumably more than one mould was made from the model), in most cases there are less than a dozen of each of the repeated creatures. The great monkey arches, for instance, sport a total of seventy-eight individual monkeys. Six of these are identical keystones, while the other eight designs are repeated nine times. However, the subtle rhythms of the repetition, and the variations in it, are part of the essence of the Museum, and we might ask who was responsible for them. Much of the richness is achieved by simple alternation of two, or three, similar shapes. This provides an A, B, A, B or A, B, C, A, B, C pattern; but Waterhouse evidently enjoyed varying this where he could. We have already noted the complex interplay between the repetition of three freestanding beasts and four gable roundels along the façade of each wing. In the case of the first-floor windows, of which there are eighteen to each wing, the pattern is more insistent, though still carefully modulated. Each wing has three different beasts to sit below the window mullion. These are flanked by relief panels, for which Waterhouse provided four designs. However, as we have seen, two of those are used to make one pair of panels, while the other two are simply repeated. The fishes of plate 53, for instance, face each other and each fish occurs six times, while the lizard and foliage of plate 54 are each repeated and twelve castings are used. The resulting rhythms, which are read in relation to the march of identical bays along the façade, sets up a series of patterns that have the same sort of intellectual satisfaction when read as systems of mathematical tiling.

It is an almost endlessly variable geometric maze; yet there are some surprising uncertainties. On the soffits of the monkey arches, for instance, there are no less than six different forms of rosette, repeated above the springing in what appears to be an almost random fashion. There are similar disturbances of the rhythm elsewhere. The cornice beasts of the west wing, as we noted, follow the rhythm A, B, C, B, A, C, A, C, B, A, C, B.[20] The break in strict order is even more apparent in the entrance, where two series of fine capitals interlock as a major and minor order (fig 79). The capitals of the major follow a regular pattern, while the minor (plate 66) has a more wilful contrasting rhythm: I, L, I, J, K, L, K. It is almost as though the capitals had been set at random, or varied according to the whim of the builder. In the case of the fourteen designs for panels on the gate piers, there is no discernible pattern beyond the fact that most are used once on the inner face and once on the outer. The share of responsibility or credit for these breaks from insistent rhythms may never be precisely defined. We know, for instance, that Waterhouse's sketches were related to another set of construction drawings to a consistent scale. Without that guidance, the modeller would have been unable to proceed at all, but most of his constructional drawings are at too small a scale for us to be certain which of his terracotta ornaments were intended for which column. The choice might even have been a decision taken on the spot. One drawing survives that is coded with references to a whole series of sheets of half-inch scale details (fig 80), but the drawing is marked 'incorrect' and is unfinished. Presumably, it was abandoned when it was found to be inaccurate in some detail. Later, it must have been resuscitated and crudely labelled with letters that would allow ready cross-reference to the drawings for the terracotta. However, the need to work from an incorrect drawing must have involved some risk of error.

One can imagine how difficult it must have been for hard-pressed staff in an office where this was merely one commission – though an important one – among many, to keep track of the sheer quantity of detailed drawings and instructions. What is little short of amazing is that Waterhouse must have held most of it in his mind. Others, such as the modeller, the builder, or the Clerk of Works,

78. A new lion and a 'mythical' replacement for the wolf of the west parapet await transport from the manufacturers, 1998. (Photo courtesy of Ibstock Hathernware Ltd)

79. Patterned shafts of the principal entrance.

80. A rough perspective, noted as 'incorrect', is used as a key to the various decorative details. A note records: 'The letters refer to the several 1/2" scale sheets. All enrichments should be drawn from the executed work at the building'. The drawing is undated, but significantly there is a suggestion, R, that 1/2" scale details exist for the ceiling painting. (Pencil, 72.5 x 53.5 cm. Courtesy of the British Architectural Library, Drawings Collection)

78 might have had difficulty in adhering to every detail of Waterhouse's vision. The rhythms and repetitions he devised will always have been a great deal easier to see in the finished work than when half walls were shrouded in scaffolding in the midst of a building site. There were in effect only two means of avoiding chaos among the plethora of different blocks. The architect's constructional drawings might show each individual block, and in some cases these might be numbered, making the building process something like executing a gigantic jig-saw puzzle. Or, and this seems to have been the case, the different types of block might be individually designed and their disposition arranged according to a set of instructions as to patterns. With this scenario, the number of copies of each block delivered on the ground would be crucial, and it would be fascinating to know what percentage was allowed for wastage. If there was any surplus at all, it would have been all too easy to use one extra of a particular pattern because its counterpart could not be found or had been broken.

We have to believe that Waterhouse, in addition to controlling the overall design and personally drawing out all the ornament, was able not only to carry in his mind the whole series of basic rhythms, but also to give instructions as to how this should be varied. Otherwise, we must thank Baker for some unintentional softening of what might have been rather insistent rhythms. It is certainly conceivable that he had instructions from Waterhouse to vary the patterns of ornamental blocks, and simply set them as they came to hand; but it seems unlikely. It is one more enigma in this most fascinating of buildings.

That such aspects of the construction are a matter of speculation is due to the fact that a great deal of archival material is lost. The Clerk of Works' notebooks, for instance, which might have filled some of the gaps, do not survive. The sketches only occasionally have a note of the quantity of blocks required. Yet the inscriptions do show that the designs were carefully scrutinised on site: many are dated and signed, but the signature is not that of Waterhouse and the dates do not record the day the drawing was done. The signature on the drawings is that of Charles Till (or his initials), who was Clerk of Works for the later half of the construction period – the period when the bulk of the terracotta ornament was being made. He seems to have been a methodical man, initialling each sketch as the model was approved. The dates are frequently give as 'sent', or sometimes 'sent to the manufacturers', on a given day. Till, who knew that there was a period of around eight weeks from delivery at the manufactory to arrival on the ground, would undoubtedly have been concerned to ensure that the models went away for making in good time. He had the responsibility of keeping Baker supplied with the appropriate blocks for the section he would be working on in two months' time. It was no simple task, but at the time of Baker's bankruptcy the charge of incompetence against Waterhouse and his staff was not sustained, so we may presume Till did well enough.[21]

His job may have been made slightly easier by Waterhouse's system of designing the various groups of blocks in series. The letter, or number, headings on the sketches show that this was how he worked. This will also have been important for the modeller. Distinguishing between the capitals of the major and minor orders of the entrance, similar in shape but different in size, would have been much easier if one could see the different series set out side by side on the modelling bench. Yet this will have created one last difficulty, which, again, Waterhouse foresaw and dealt with. The material, as I have said, was still to some extent experimental, and the dates of some of the series suggest that Waterhouse was anxious to go slowly and test things out. One large and one small panel of the fourteen for the great staircase, for instance, were 'sent' on 4 September 1878 (plates 88 & 91). The rest were all sent in two batches on 30 October and 20 December.[22] The gap strongly suggests that Waterhouse or Till was arranging for trial specimens and waiting for the return of the finished blocks in each case before sending batches of the precious models away.

Where Waterhouse and Owen and the various keepers share the credit for the accuracy, or otherwise, of many of the creatures, the satisfactory reproduction of the designs rested partly on the organisational skills of Till and Baker, partly on the reliability of Gibbs and Canning, but most of all on the team of craftsmen who produced the models. Dujardin was certainly the key to that, and while Waterhouse, as creative designer, had the role of ringmaster to the whole circus, Dujardin deserves to be remembered for the achievement. It is also clear from the few references available that Waterhouse and most other critics thought of him as a sculptor, not merely a mechanical modeller. Thus, his role, and the freedom Waterhouse allowed him in modelling from single small sketches, becomes extremely important. Waterhouse's early study of Gothic mouldings had given him a precise understanding of the effects of the shadows cast by mouldings of different shapes and depths.

But he had never before chosen such a hazardous path, nor aimed at so rich an ornamental effect. He was never to do so again, but it is small wonder that in 1893, almost twenty-five years after he had received the commission, he chose his perspective of The Natural History Museum as one of two exhibits to represent him, as a leading architect of Europe, at the Chicago World's Fair. If Dujardin had crossed the Atlantic and was modelling terracotta for the likes of Louis Sullivan, it is to be hoped that he visited the exhibition and remembered this job with pride.

Notes

1 Alfred Waterhouse to First Commissioner of Works, 20 Nov 1871, PRO Work 17 16/3.

2 Alfred Waterhouse to First Commissioner of Works, 19 Dec 1871, PRO Work 17 16/3.

3 Alfred Waterhouse to First Commissioner of Works, 20 Nov 1871, PRO Work 17 16/3.

4 PRO Work 17 16/3. Ms letter AW to First Commissioner of Works, 27 May 1873. Messrs Bunnett & Co subsequently had minor contracts under Waterhouse at Owens College in Manchester and in the redevelopment of Cooks Court, Carey Street. Hodkinson, presumably of the firm of Lester & Hodkinson, had no work from him after 1871. BJ Morris does not reappear in the Waterhouse archive. The models in question were probably only for simple moulded blocks, but would have given an indication of the level of skill available.

5 Emma Hardy, 'Farmer & Brindley: Craftsman Sculptors 1850–1930', Pevsner Memorial Prize essay, *Victorian Society Annual*, 1994, p4.

6 See Kelly's *Post Office Directory*, 1870.

7 See Carla Yanni, 'Divine Display or Secular Science: Defining Nature at the Natural History Museum in London., in *Journal of the Society of Architectural Historians*, vol 55, no3 September, 1996, p298, n 66.

8 See, for instance, Kelly's Post Office Directories for 1865 and 1874. Two other Dujardins are known in the London area from the 1881 Census (the only one to have a complete surname index) – Henry Dujardin, a carpenter in St Pancras and Aglae Louise, a French teacher in Carshalton. It has not been possible to prove a relationship with any of these, though the surname is unusual enough to allow speculation.

9 Waterhouse's sketchbooks reveal that he was in Paris in April 1870.

10 See 1881 Census, surname index. Michael Stratton, *The Terra Cotta Revival*, Gollancz, London, 1993, shows how extensive was the transatlantic traffic in craftsmen in the industry.

11 *The Building News*, vol 30, 4 February 1876, p111.

12 *The Building News*, vol 30, 11 February 1876, p157.

13 *The Building News*, vol 30, 25 February 1876, p210.

14 The public inauguration in 1860 of Oxford University Museum was the occasion for the famous debate between TH Huxley and Bishop 'Soapy Sam' Wilberforce about the Darwinian theory of evolution.

15 RIBA Drawings Collection, Wat [56].

16 At least two models would be needed for these monograms, for a note on the drawing states that the letters are 'to be gilt on the face & Every other monogram to read the contrary way'. RIBA Drawings Collection, Wat [56].

17 In this context it is worth remembering that the outer walls of the building were of load-bearing brick, into which the terracotta blocks had to be keyed. In addition, alternate blocks of the plain walling were no more than tiles, 2 inches thick, cemented to the surface and relying for their stability on the accurate fitting of the larger terracotta blocks around them.

18 For a detailed study of the damage, see Caroline Dear, 'Terra Cotta at the Natural History Museum', Bournemouth University School of Conservation Sciences, BSc dissertation, 1998.

19 See Stratton, *The Terra Cotta Revival*, op. cit.

20 The rhythm is made even more complex for today's viewer by the fact that, the nice continuation of a system that Waterhouse and his builder began has been disrupted, one of the beasts has been replaced and the new cast has been made to face in the opposite direction to the other examples of that design.

21 It is tempting to believe that Till's predecessor in the job, Farquharson, may have left because he did not give the same satisfaction. Perhaps it was even he who allowed the earlier sketches to be destroyed.

22 It is assumed that the date '1877' on plate 93 is an error.

VI
an ornamental creation

81. View of the first-floor gallery and upper stair in the Museum, 1881. (H Dixon, The Natural History Museum Archives)

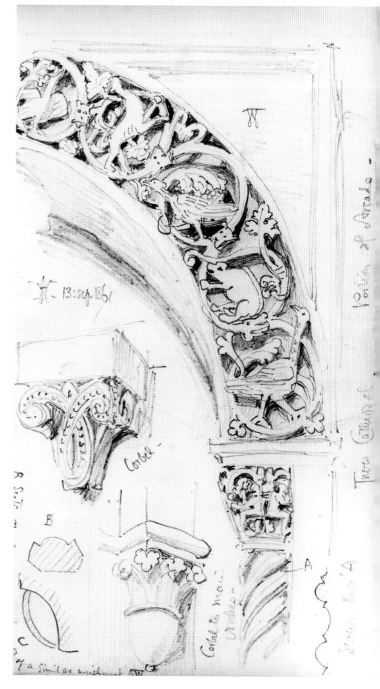

82. The ornamental portal of Trêves Cathedral, sketched in September 1861, is a clear source of inspiration for the many images of birds and beasts in foliage that Waterhouse used in his terracotta designs. (SB IV. 9, 10.5 x 16.5 cm. Private Collection)

"The Building is not a Classical one, although it has classical traditions in its balanced symmetry... Nor is it a Romanesque building, notwithstanding the varying recurrence of the round arch. It is not a Gothic building though having steep gables and an arrangement of roofing which are eminently Gothic in motif, as they are effective and picturesque in outline and grouping. It is, in short, a Victorian building and no other, designed upon principles which have informed the great works of all time, but adapted to the wants, using the materials and employing the methods of the age in which we live."[1]

This quotation from the *Magazine of Art* is typical of the praise for the completed structure, couched largely in architectural terms and focusing on the form of the building rather than its decoration. And it was, most definitely, an architectural masterpiece (fig 81). As late as 1900, it was cited by the French theorist Leon Lefêvre as the only British example to illustrate his study of pottery in architecture. He described it as 'a vast construction entirely built of stone-coloured brick, which is left uncovered both outside and inside. The general effect is most imposing'.[2]

Scientists, on the whole, were dismissive of the building and its ornament, for their interest was emphatically in the displays it housed, rather than the Museum itself. By the time the Museum was opened in 1881, Darwin's *On the Origin of Species* had been published for over twenty years. Science had moved on from Owen's cautious conservatism and it was fashionable to criticise the building in the light of contemporary scientific enquiry. This was hardly fair in an age before the concept of flexible planning, and, in any case, ignored the simple fact that Britain had at last acquired a central building capable of showing to the public the results of current endeavour in the natural sciences. If it was not perfect, it was at least a very major advance on the situation of the mid-century.

The castigation of the building for its old-fashioned creationist display was in part a continuing attack on the ageing Richard Owen, pilloried for a decision taken twenty years before for a scheme of decoration that was in any case never defined in any precisely pedagogic way. Although Owen had suggested from the start that 'many objects of natural history might afford subjects for architectural ornament',[3] there is no suggestion that he wanted the decoration to be a precise illustration of the contents of his Museum. He had, however, approved Waterhouse's choice

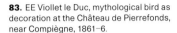
83. EE Viollet le Duc, mythological bird as decoration at the Château de Pierrefonds, near Compiègne, 1861–6.

84. William Burges and Thomas Nicholls, animal wall at Cardiff Castle, 1887–8.

of Romanesque Gothic, which was especially suited to rich decoration. 'No style could better lend itself to the introduction, for legitimate ornamentation, of the endless beautiful varieties of form and surface sculpture exemplified in the animal and vegetable kingdoms'.[4] In short, the Museum and its decoration stood firmly within the tradition of Romanesque and Gothic animal decoration that had its own roots in the imagined creatures of early Christian bestiaries as much as in actual observation.

Scientific description played no part in that symbolic medieval world, but the bestiaries gave rise to a rich crop of decorative beasts (fig 82) and Waterhouse was by no means the only architect of the Gothic revival to draw on it as ornamental source material. The great French rationalist, Viollet le Duc, had enriched the reconstructed castle of Pierrefonds (1859–70) with exotic beasts that derived straight from medieval mythology (fig 83); while William Burges, inspired by the drawings of the thirteenth-century Villard de Honnecourt, had designed a series of extraordinarily life-like escaping beasts to complete the wall of his medieval dream castle at Cardiff (fig 83). By the mid-nineteenth century, scientific observation was important in ensuring that the images depicted by the revivalists were recognisable. Far away in India, when Waterhouse's Museum was barely complete, Colonel Frederick Stevens was drawing on the real riches of Indian flora and fauna to decorate the grandest railway station of the Raj (fig 85). These are representative contemporary examples demonstrating the same suitability for ornament that was felt to be integral to Waterhouse's revived Romanesque. Yet Waterhouse appears to have drawn equally on both aspects of the tradition. Not only did he include naturalistic portrayals of

85. FW Stevens and sculptors of the Jamsetjee Jeejeebhoy School of Art; monkey capital from Victoria Terminus (Chhatrapati Shivaji Terminus), Bombay, India, 1878-87.

Any assessment of the building and its ornament needs to take into account comparable iconographies. Other scientific museums, notably the Oxford University Museum and the Museum of Science and Art in Edinburgh are natural precedents. The latter, by Francis Fowke, the original designer of The Natural History Museum, may have seemed especially important, but it lacks the rich ornamental overlay of the metropolitan building. The Oxford building, more a science centre than a museum, has a strongly didactic foundation for its decoration, which presents geological and plant specimens as exemplars of God's creation. As Carla Yanni has pointed out,[5] 'its Gothic architecture stresses the way that science in Oxford was presented as a continuing manifestation of Christian wonder at the divine ordering of the natural world'. The Natural History Museum is different. The unfortunate decision to separate extinct from living species was a historically bound choice that proved outdated; but it was at least a scientific choice. The Museum did attempt to link actual science in its organisation and its decoration. However, I believe it also attempted a great deal more, and should be seen alongside that other iconographical extravaganza of South Kensington, the Albert Memorial.

When Prince Albert died in 1862, he was commemorated in a monument that not only encapsulates all the Christian and moral virtues, all the sciences and the Arts, but which also makes sweeping claims to world supremacy in the way in which it is supported by sculptural groups representing the Four Quarters of the Globe. It is aspirational whilst being in many ways conventional. It was also the focal point of the Albertopolis development, of which The Natural History Museum itself was a key element. Something of those assumptions of conventional Christianity can be seen in The Natural History Museum, where the statue of Adam, as the most highly developed of the primates and God's finest creation, tops the central gable. Interestingly, one early design allowed for two statues, Adam and Eve, side by side, a representation of male and female that would have been entirely suitable for a

creatures and plants, he also returned to the locus classicus of Romanesque architecture, sketching foliage and creatures on capitals for St Trophîme at Arles at the very moment he was beginning his designs for The Natural History Museum ornament (fig 86). It is this reach into two related types of source material that gives his ornament its richness and which goes furthest to explain his intentions.

Owen's much despised creationism certainly played a part. Yet there was so much more to the decoration of this extraordinary building, and it seems likely that, as the dated nature of Owen's rigid distinction between extinct and living species became increasingly apparent and more widely acknowledged, Waterhouse availed himself of the opportunity to soften the division. It was a system that in any case only applied to the wings of the Museum, but it is surely significant that by the time the roof cresting was fitted, Waterhouse felt free to use the same seven designs for both wings, reserving only the pterodactyl for the east wing. Waterhouse availed himself of similar flexibility inside. It is, for instance, curious that bats are reserved for the pilasters of the extinct wing only, when it was well known that there were many living species of bats. In addition, there were major decorative elements in the Index Museum and the Museum of British Natural History that were, by definition, outside Owen's creationist division. The iconography of the whole is both more complex and more uncertain.

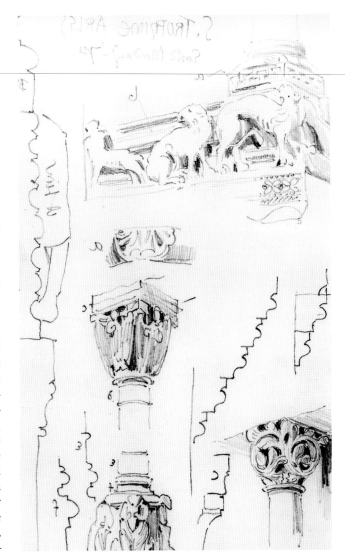

84

museum of natural history. The decision to choose Adam alone suggests that the architectural imperative of a central gable was the driving force rather than the most appropriate scientific statement.

Beyond the obvious, but ultimately blurred, distinction between extinct and living species, one looks in vain for a clear symbolism that covers the whole Museum. It is easy enough to divide the ornament into three categories: the abstract, the formalised and the naturalistic. The two former types are most easily dismissed as purely decorative, driven by the desire to create pattern. This division is supported by the fact that only two such decorative elements have species identified. The more carefully naturalistic portrayals, then, are more susceptible to a symbolic interpretation, but one looks in vain for clear and comprehensive evidence of this. Fourteen species on the gate piers, five panels over the entrance door, four roundels in the Index Museum and fourteen more on the great stair: these are not obvious groupings that can be readily translated into geographical distribution, patterns of habitat, or a hierarchy of orders of creation. There is not even a clear recognition of the different areas of study or even the orders of zoology. Geology is almost completely absent, herpetology and entomology largely ignored and ichthyology barely represented. Botany, on the other hand, is perhaps over-represented in the gallery piers and the ceiling panels, though the latter could be excused as an afterthought. If Waterhouse was looking for firm direction from his client, he certainly did not find it, which in turn suggests that the living/extinct division may have been less important for Owen, at least as far as the ornament was concerned.

One can look for other parameters, but there is no certainty. The political role of the Museum might need to be considered. It was a considerable achievement and a demonstration of the civilisation of Britain as a leading Western nation. Though we have learned to doubt such views today, it may well be that this sort of cultural supremacy, something that a Victorian would have accepted without question, finds some reflection in the building. Such a view could explain the iconography of the entrance portal. Entrances were recognised as particularly symbolic and we may legitimately wonder how far Waterhouse attempted to make the moment of entry into this Cathedral of Science a special one. It is possible that he made a typically Victorian attempt to demonstrate world coverage with specimens from five continents in the panels over the doorway. In his

designs, the North American black bear is carefully named, and there is a kangaroo for Australasia. The jaguar, from its range as far south as Paraguay could be taken as representing South America, while the spotted hyena would stand for Africa. Asia, however, is not represented, though this could be because the conventional beast, used on the Albert Memorial, was the elephant which would be ruled out here on grounds of scale. Besides, Asia, in the form of the British Raj, was not seen as a source of natural history so much as of material wealth and Mughal culture. The central panel, which by elimination ought to represent Europe, displays a lioness encircled by a particularly fierce and large-headed snake. A nineteenth-century viewer might easily have read this as a Europe in which civilisation (the lion for its royal and heraldic associations, the female of the species for connotations of home and family) fought with the powers of darkness. If such an interpretation is accepted, it is hardly natural history, though it is undeniably decorative and solves the problem of a centrally arranged middle panel, with the 'lesser' continents facing inwards from each side. The final touch is the pair of heads peering from the spandrels over the window. No one in the late 1870s would have been surprised to find the building making some claim to British superiority in the carefully identified bulldog, though it is not a particularly convincing portrait. Equally, by the same date, the majority of the scientific community would have accepted a reference to the ascending order of primates, with the monkey, here an anonymous species, as the most highly developed of the animals.

There is, of course, no proof that this slightly confused message was intended. It is inherently unlikely that the scientist in Owen would have been interested in the political message. Equally, Waterhouse had no reputation as a deviser of elaborate iconographical schemes. However, there must at some point have been a choice of which species to present at such a significant place on the building and it seems entirely possible that the double message of the four continents and the triumph of civilisation were both felt acceptable.

There is a similar difficulty in explaining the four great roundels in the gallery of the Index Museum. One looks for some world reference in a space devoted to a summary display of world natural history. Yet the heron and the ibex are both European species, while the mazama and the rhea are South American. If the division is that of 'home' and 'abroad', Europe can be taken as the familiar home world, but the choice of South America is something of an enigma. Just possibly, it is an acknowledgement of the new discoveries there by Darwin on the first stage of the Beagle voyage. In which case, the Museum's recognition of the new science goes further than has been recognised hitherto. But the message of the Index Museum, if there really is one, is far from clear. Stencilled on the gallery ceiling are a series of small images of birds, plants, a scorpion, reptiles and marine creatures that defy any coherent iconographical explanation (fig 87). Their random arrangement is in marked contrast to the careful, and carefully labelled, didacticism of the painted ceiling, which was designed at the same time, and executed by the same firm (figs 88 & 89).

On the whole, it seems more likely that there are several levels of reference at work. Broadly, the generic reference seems the most consistent and widespread. However, there are also attempts at relevance, for instance in the choice of the dodo for the tympanum of the extinct galleries. Nineteenth-century men of science were well aware that this species had been driven to extinction relatively recently by Dutch sailors.[6] Its presence on the walls of the Museum was, therefore, not so much a statement of the fact that it was extinct, as a comment on the importance of the Museum and of scientific study in the battle for preservation of other threatened species. By the same token, the regular appearance of owls, of one species or another, can be read as a general reference to wisdom and learning. There seems to be a range of such merely generic reference. The monkeys on the Entrance Hall arches (fig 90) are often taken as an acknowledgement of Darwinian theories, and no doubt Waterhouse would have accepted that interpretation. However, they are equally likely to be intended as recognition of the hierarchy of species. Finally, they are perhaps the most appropriate species to be depicted climbing the airy mouldings of the arches. In the same way, the twined snakes of the archway between the west gallery and the north corridor may be both a suitable running ornament for the hollow of an arch, and a reference to the biblical serpent of the Garden of Eden.

In short, we probably have to admit that there was no controlling orthodoxy behind the decorative scheme. The driving force seems more likely to have been simply the urge to adorn, and Waterhouse's motivation to have been that of pattern and scale rather than any complicated intellectual exercise. The division into abstract and formalised images on the one hand and naturalistic portrayals on the other, can be seen as no more than an acceptance that there were places when it would be appropriate to include representations of species alongside the patterns he had created out of natural forms. The key factor in the choice of species may itself have been simply a matter of scale and the ease with which a given creature could be disposed to fill a panel (fig 91).

On this analysis, we are free simply to enjoy the models for their own sake, and to share in the same aesthetic pleasure that undoubtedly fed Waterhouse's desire to sketch every design himself. If, ultimately, there is no hidden intellectual knot for us to disentangle, we should simply accept that these images are extraordinarily varied and we should not cavil at the invitation merely to enjoy and wonder at a creative imagination that mixed pattern and naturalism with such facility (fig 92).

86

87. A section of unrestored ceiling on the first floor of the Entrance Hall, with stencilled images of various creatures and plants. (The Natural History Museum, Picture Library)

88. Panel from the ceiling of the Index Museum painted by Charles James Lea: the lemon (*Citrus limonum*). (The Natural History Museum, Picture Library)

89. Panel from the ceiling of the Index Museum painted by Charles James Lea: the cocoa plant (*Theobroma cacao*). (The Natural History Museum, Picture Library)

Opposite page:
90. A view of the three monkey arches of the Index Museum and Entrance Hall.

88

91. Panel of demoiselle cranes from the principal staircase (see plate 89).

92. Panel of the great owl from the gate piers (see plate 13).

Notes

1 *The Magazine of Art*, vol 4, 1881, p36.

2 Leon Lefêvre, *Architectural Pottery*, Scott Greenwood & Son, London, 1900.

3 Richard Owen, quoted in Rev R Owen, *The Life of Richard Owen*, John Murray, London, 1894, p50.

4 Ibid., p52.

5 Carla Yanni, 'Nature as Creation', Chapter 3 in *Nature's Museums: Victorian Science and the Architecture of Display*, Athlone Press, London, 1999.

6 See HE Strickland & AG Melville, *The Dodo and its Kindred or the History, Affinity, and Osteology of the Dodo, Solitaire, and other Extinct Birds of the Island Mauritius*, Rodriguez and Bourbon, London, 1848. I am grateful to Carla Yanni for this suggestion.

The sizes given for the drawings are in all cases of the whole sheet; however, where a substantial area is left blank only the drawn image has been reproduced.

1 Six blocks of unidentified birds and foliage for the jambs of the arches in the Index Museum, with details for a rosette for the soffit of the arches that support the stair, and a simple small capital used elsewhere in the Museum. Unusually, this drawing also includes a section of the blocks showing how the ribs are to be moulded, but not how the foliage or birds are to be managed. (vol I.1, 24 Nov, 24 Dec 1874. 26.5 x 37.5 cm)

2 Eight blocks for the voussoirs of the arches in the Index Museum with five different designs for birds and three, including the keystone, with foliage only. The foliage is based on a Romanesque detail that Waterhouse sketched in Arles. (vol I.2, 20 Nov 1874. 26.5 x 37.5 cm)

90

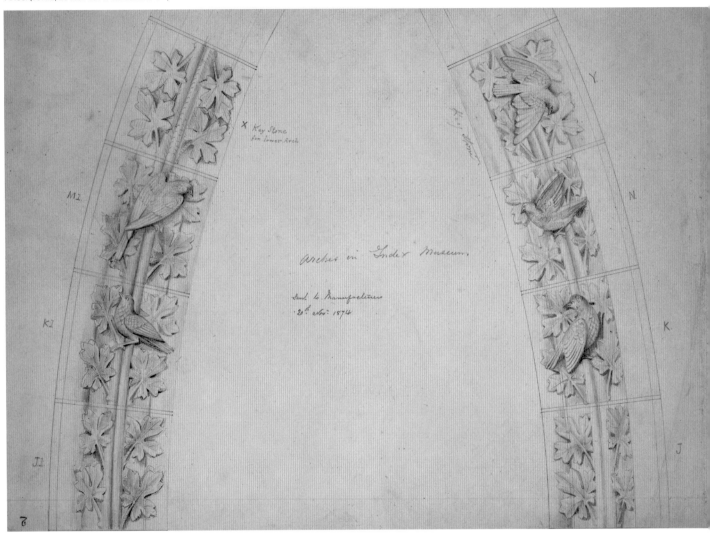

3 Designs for ten pieces of the main arches of the Index Museum have four different versions of 'Darwinian' monkeys and plain sections of a climbing stem, which are repeated. Below are sections of the architectural ribs on to which the models are grafted. The sheet shows indentations on monkey F, which may indicate that Waterhouse was experimenting with moving the head to the left to give the effect of a monkey peering round the column. (vol I.3, 24 Nov 1874. 37.5 x 26.5 cm)

4 Five further versions of the monkeys for the main arches. There are nine different designs in all, including the keystone, which face alternately to right and left. Each monkey is made from two blocks of terracotta with a joint at the waist, carefully pointed to match the colour of the clay body. The monkeys were more widely spaced than is suggested by this design, see figure 55. (vol I.4, 5 Jan 1875. 26.5 x 37.5 cm)

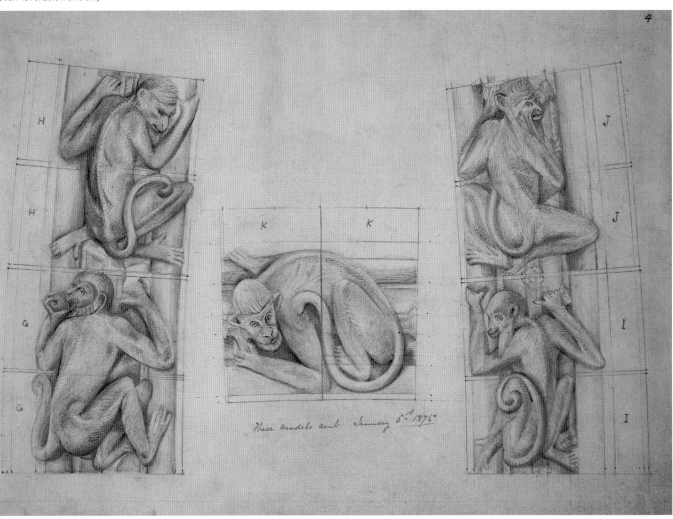

5 One of the set of fifteen panels for the gate piers of the south front, A, shows the cobra, 'The Haje of Egypt'. (vol II.35. 27 x 37 cm)

6 One of the set of fifteen panels for the gate piers of the south front, B, shows the weasel (*Mustela vulgaris*). (vol II.36. 27 x 37 cm)

7 One of the set of fifteen panels for the gate piers of the south front, C, shows the brown sajou (*Cebus apella*). (vol II.37. 27 x 37.5 cm)

8 One of the set of fifteen panels for the gate piers of the south front, D, shows the smooth-necked iguana (*Iguana nudicollis*). (vol II.38. 27 x 37.5 cm)

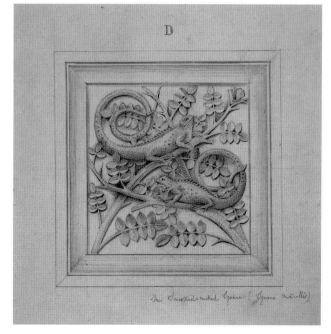

9 One of the set of fifteen panels for the gate piers of the south front, E, shows the Senegal galago (*Galago senegalensis*). (vol II.39. 27 x 37 cm)

10 One of the set of fifteen panels for the gate piers of the south front, F, shows the passenger pigeon (*Ectopistes migratorius*). (vol II.40. 27 x 37.5 cm)

11 One of the set of fifteen panels for the gate piers of the south front, G, shows a pair of asps. (vol II.41. 27 x 37.5 cm)

12 One of the set of fifteen panels for the gate piers of the south front, H, shows the hen harrier (*Circus cyaneus*). (vol II.42. 27 x 37.5 cm)

13 One of the set of fifteen panels for the gate piers of the south front, I, shows the great owl (*Bubo maximus*). (vol II.43. 27 x 37 cm)

14 One of the set of fifteen panels for the gate piers of the south front, J, shows a pair of black rats (*Mus rattus*). (vol II.44. 27 x 37 cm)

15 One of the set of fifteen panels for the gate piers of the south front, K, shows the scaled fruit crow (*Coracina scutata*). (vol II.45. 27 x 36.5 cm)

16 One of the set of fifteen panels for the gate piers of the south front, L, shows the red squirrel (*Sciurus vulgaris*). (vol II.46. 27 x 37 cm)

17 One of the set of fifteen panels for the gate piers of the south front, M, shows the Alexandrine parakeet (*Palaeornis alexandri*). (vol II.47. 27 x 37.5 cm)

18 One of the set of fifteen panels for the gate piers of the south front, N, shows the pied wagtail (*Motacilla yarelli*), and is the only one of this series to be dated. (vol II.48. 20 Nov 1878. 27 x 37.5 cm)

96

19 One of the set of fifteen panels for the gate piers of the south front, O, shows a group of garden warblers (*Curruca hortensis*). (vol II.49. 27 x 37.5 cm)

20 Preliminary drawing for a panel, presumably for the gate piers. Such a drawing would almost certainly have been prepared by one of the office draughtsmen for Waterhouse to work on. (vol II.33. 27 x 37.5 cm)

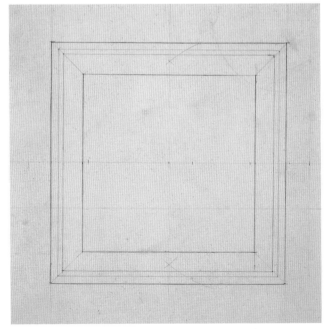

21 A further uncompleted design for one of the gate piers (cf plate 20). It may be that Waterhouse intended to introduce further creatures, but was prevented either by lack of time or lack of finance. (vol II.50. 27 x 37 cm)

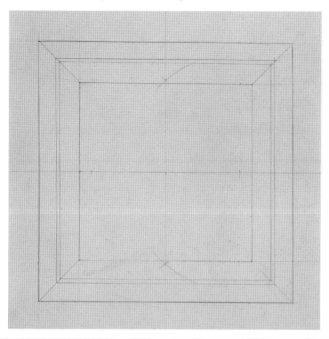

22 Gargoyle for the south gallery cornice. Waterhouse does not specify whether this is intended for the east wing, with its extinct species, or for the living ones of the west wing. (vol I.49, 18 May 1876. 26.5 x 37.5 cm)

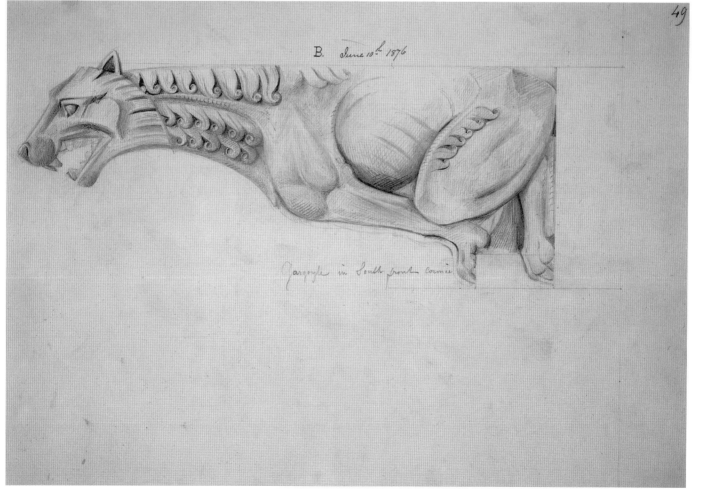

23 Another gargoyle for the south front cornice, and again the wing is not specified. (vol I.48, 10 Jun 1876. 26.5 x 37.5 cm)

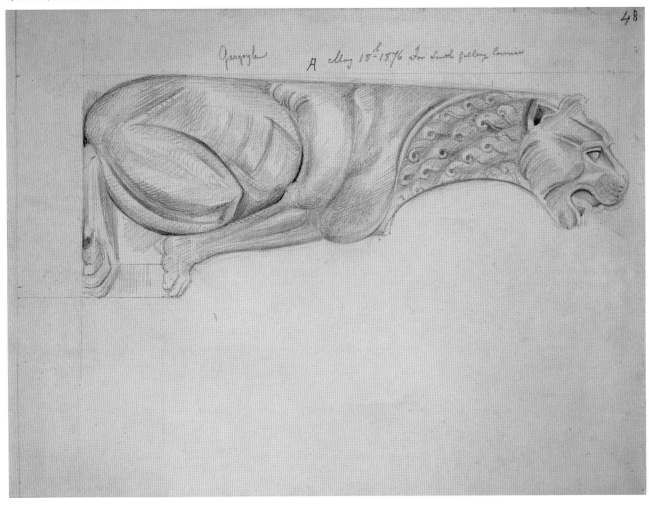

24 Waterhouse's design for the dog (*Canis*), A, for one of the roundels in the gables of the west wing of the south front, shows how skilfully he adapted the animals to the circular frame, even if the breed of dog is indeterminate. It is one of a series labelled A to G. (vol I.52, 2 Jun 1876. 26.5 x 37.5 cm)

25 The goat (*Caper hircus*) roundel B, for a gable in the west wing of the south front is one of Waterhouse's most lively and successful designs, combining realistic depiction with a strong sense of design. (vol I.53, 2 Jun 1876. 26.5 x 37.5 cm)

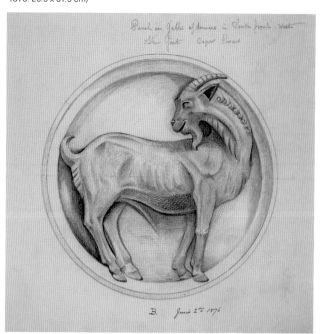

26 The fox (*Vulpes vulgaris*) roundel, C in the series, is recognisable enough, though one might feel its nose was on the short side and more could have been made of its brush. It is nonetheless a fine piece of pencil-work, and was designed to be seen from some fifty feet below. (vol I.54. 2 Jun 1876. 26.5 x 37.5 cm)

27 The sweeping wings of the eagle D, nicely fill the circle of its gable on the east and west wings of the south front. (vol I.55, 1 Jul 1876. 26.5 x 37.5 cm)

28 Roundel E of the east wing of the south front is filled with a design of the pterodactyl (*Pterodactylus*), one of relatively few creatures from the age of the dinosaurs illustrated on the façade of the building. (vol I.56, 1 Jul 1876. 26.5 x 37.5 cm)

29 Another extinct species, *Xiphodon gracilis*, makes a particularly effective design in its roundel for the east wing of the south front. (vol I.57, 13 Jul 1876. 26.5 x 37.5 cm)

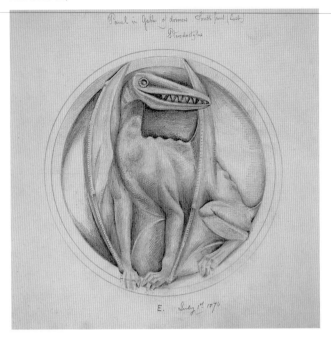

30 The palaeotherium, G in the series for the gables of the east wing, was a species in which Richard Owen had a particular interest, and is correspondingly carefully finished. (vol I.58, 13 Jul 1876. 26.5 x 37.5 cm)

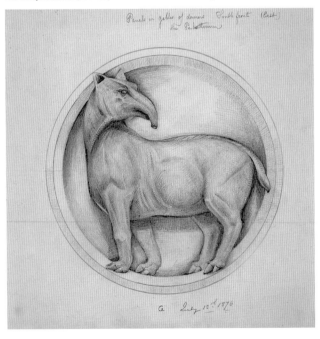

31 Three of a series of seven animals that stand on the balustrades and gables of the pavilions. Each is slightly different, but they are repeated, since a set of twelve is required for each pavilion. Each is separately signed off by the Clerk of Works and was sent to the manufacturers on a different date. (vol I.79, 23 & 30 Jun, 24 Jul 1877. 26.5 x 37.5 cm)

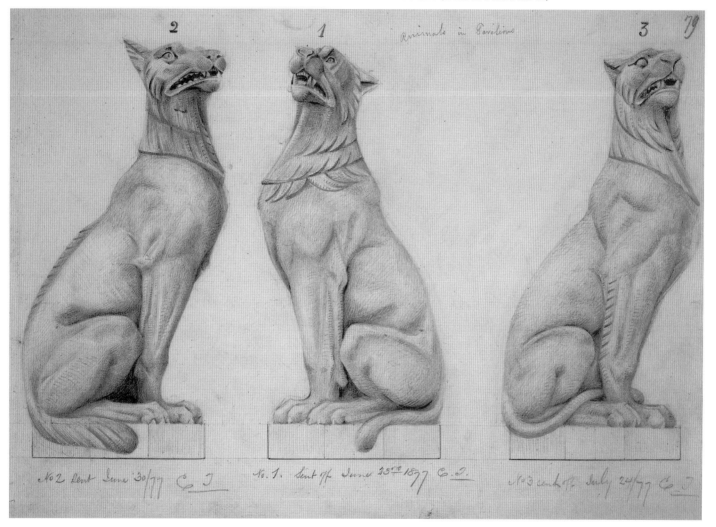

32 Two further animals for the pavilions (no 5 is listed 'gables' and copies are set on the apex of the gables that do not terminate in chimneys), signed off by the Clerk of Works, C Till, and sent at different dates (vol I.80, 8 Aug, 10 Sept 1877. 26.5 x 37.5 cm)

102

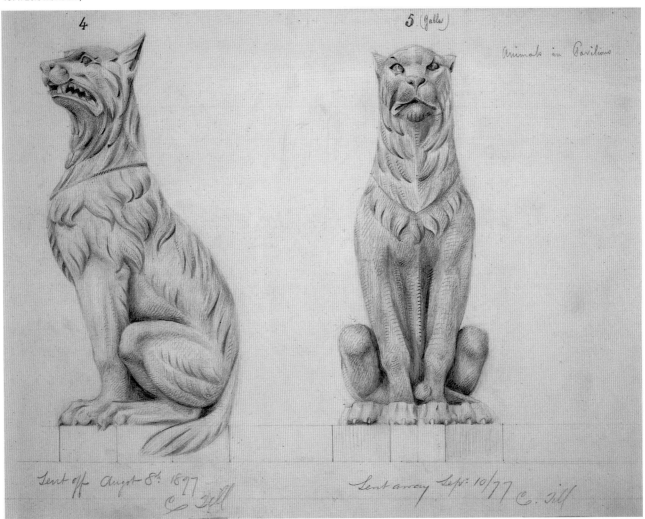

33 Front and side view of a dog and front view of the eagle (nos 6 & 7 in the series, see plates 31 & 32) for the gables of the pavilions. Both are signed by the Clerk of Works. (vol II.17, 30 Mar, 16 Apr 1878. 27 x 37 cm)

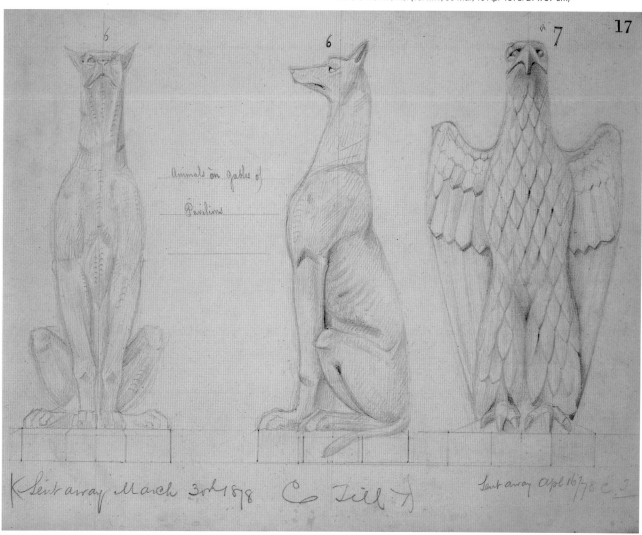

34 A larger pierced plaster vent, which is used in the ceiling of the second-floor galleries of the Entrance Hall (see also plate 79); and a side view of the eagle for the gables of the pavilions. (vol II.16. 27 x 37 cm)

35 The wolf, one of a series of six colossal creatures, labelled A–F, to stand between the dormers on the parapet of the building. This one was for the western galleries (vol I.69, 24 Aug 1876. 37.5 x 26.5 cm)

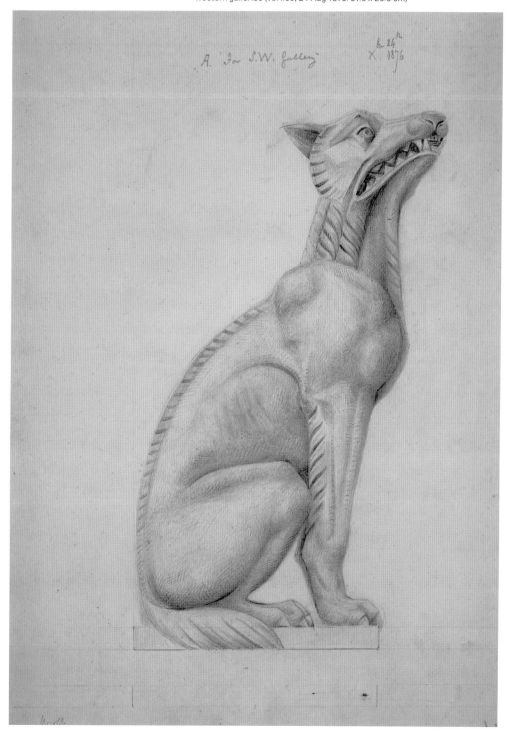

36 The lion, B in the series for the parapet. (vol I.71, 16 Apr 1877. 37.5 x 26.5 cm)

37 The panther, C in the series of creatures for the western parapet. This is dated January 1877, but a note adds 'new head sent away Feby 15 1878 CT'. It can be seen from the drawing that the new head was drawn with smaller ears. (vol I.70, 26 Jan 1877. 37.5 x 26.5 cm)

38 First labelled merely 'Sci T Lion', this creature, D in the
series for the parapet and destined for the eastern wing, is further
identified as '*Machairodus* or Scimitar Toothed Lion'. (vol I.72,
14 Feb 1877. 37.5 x 26.5 cm)

108

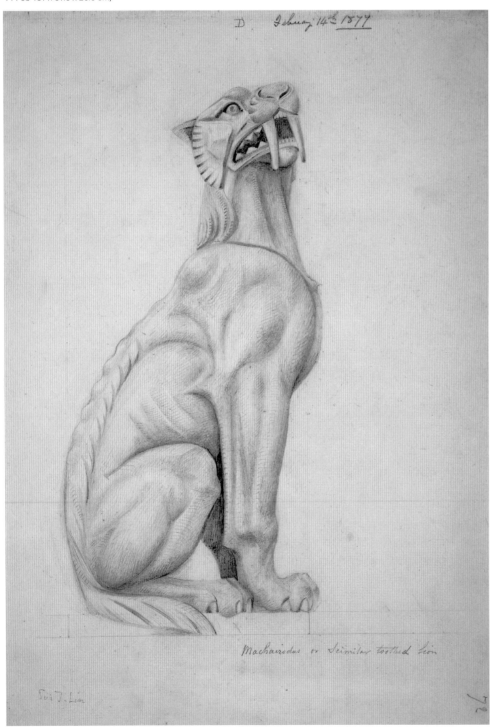

39 The mylodon, E in the series for the parapet and also for the east wing. (vol I.74, 2 May 1877. 37.5 x 26.5 cm)

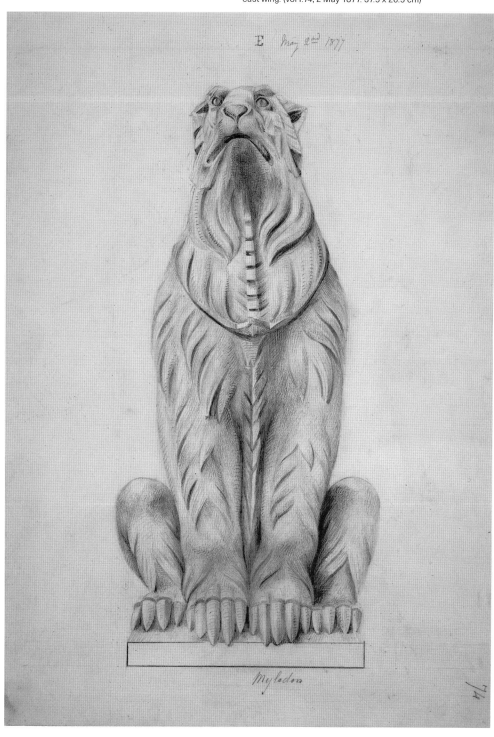

E   May 2nd 1877

Mylodon

74

40 The Great Palaeotherium, F in the series for the parapet and destined for the east wing, also occurred in a roundel in one of the gables of this wing, see plate 30. (vol I.73, 1 Mar 1877. 37.5 x 26.5 cm)

110

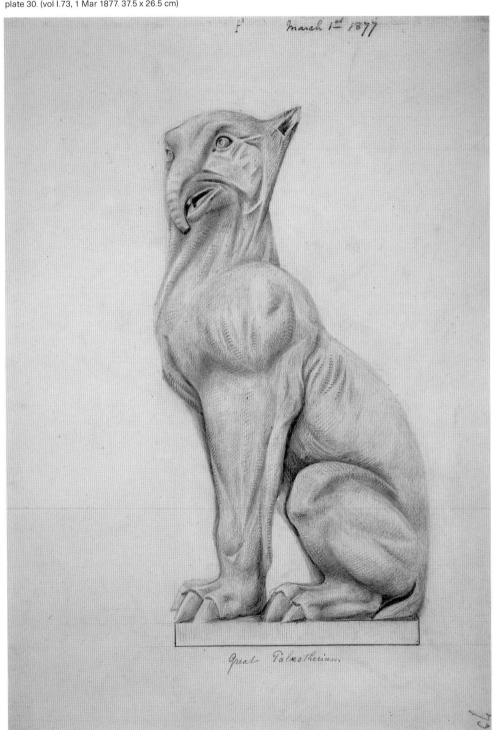

Great Palaeotherium.

41 A lion-head gargoyle for the lunettes to the pavilions. The sheet also bears faint traces of two ornamental units similar to those for the soffit of the monkey arches shown on plate 83. (vol I.44, 10 May 1875. 26.5 x 37.5 cm)

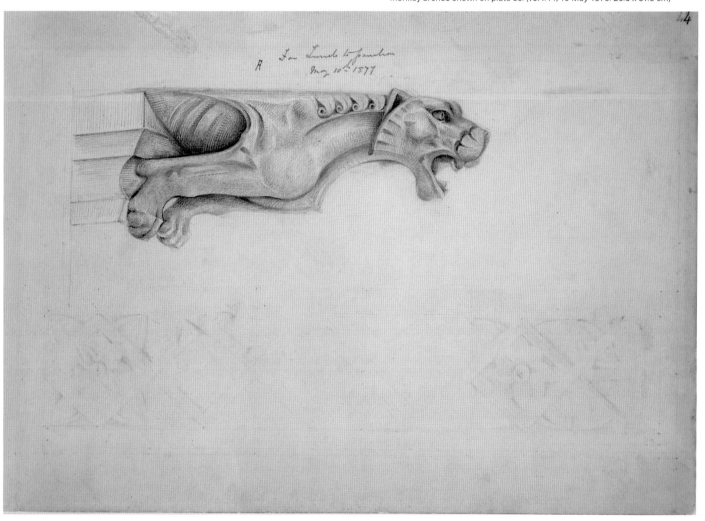

42 A revised design for a terracotta finial for the turrets in the angles of the pavilions. This design was revised yet again by Dujardin (see fig 8). Also a series of four designs for pierced florets to be made in *carton pierre*, a type of fibrous plaster. Those labelled A–C are specified as 'ventilating panels to the east gallery 2nd floor'. The sheet is signed by the Clerk of Works, C Till. (vol II.15, 23 Jan 1878. 27 x 37.5 cm)

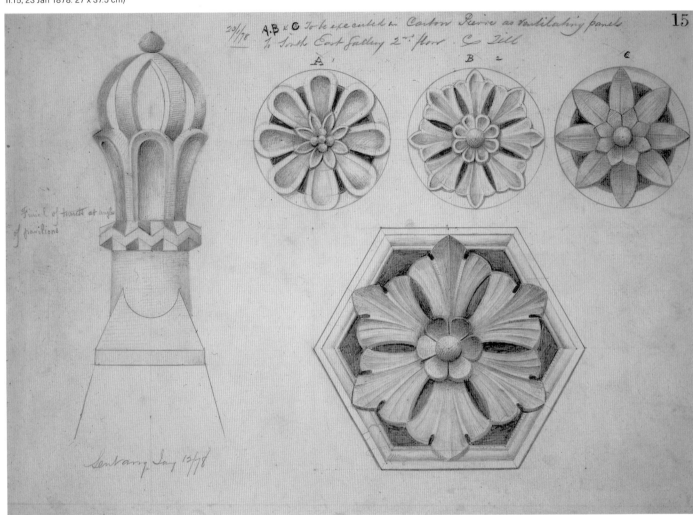

43 Simple abstract capitals based on formalised foliage, a triple one for the second-floor windows of the south central towers and a single one for the third-floor windows of the pavilions. This is labelled D & E, E being 'sent for the other hand but not sketched being exactly similar', together with a bear's-head keystone for the apex to the gable in the Entrance Hall. (vol I.66, 28 Sept 1876, 27 Apr 1877. 26.5 x 37.5 cm)

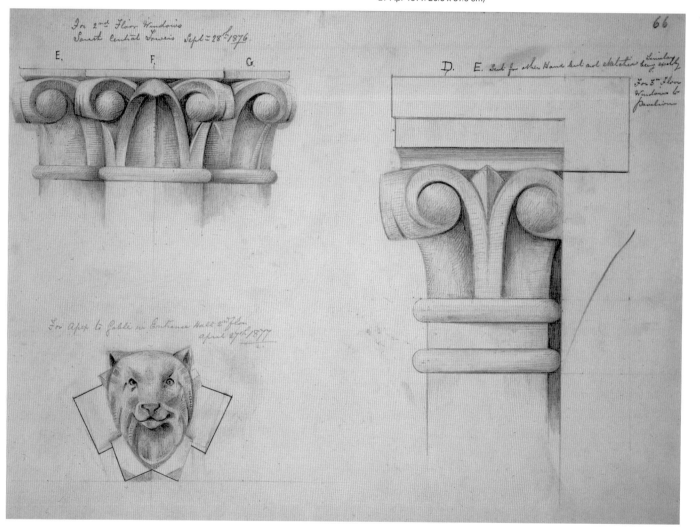

44 A further detail of a triple capital identical to one in plate 43, presumably also for the third-floor windows of the pavilions. The faces are labelled A, B and C, where the side view in plate 43 is labelled D & E. (vol I.68. 26.5 x 37.5 cm)

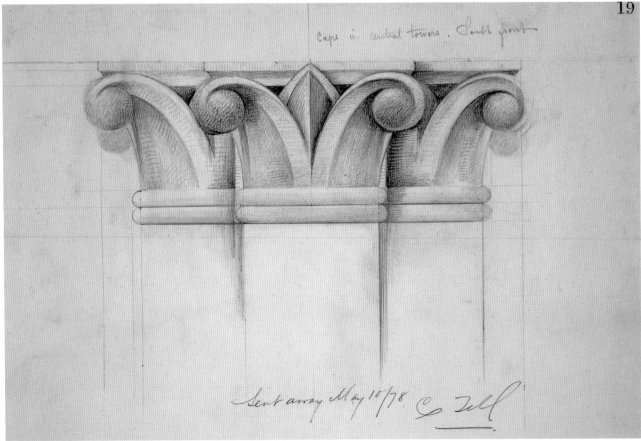

45 Design for a triple capital in the central towers of the south front, similar, but not identical, to those for the third-floor windows of the pavilions. The sheet is signed by the Clerk of Works, C Till. (vol II.19, 10 May 1878. 27 x 37 cm)

46 A triple capital and a left-handed and right-handed single capital for the sixth floor of the south towers, signed by the Clerk of Works, (vol II.23, 17 Jul 1878. 27 x 37 cm)

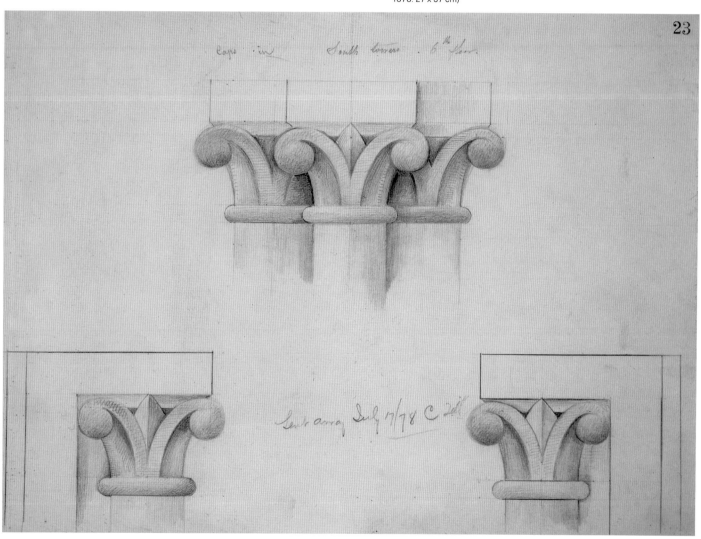

47 Further simple capitals and shafts without an identified location were probably for the upper parts of the pavilions. They are drawn together with two cornice blocks for the porter's lodge and a small lion's head, whose location is not given. Two of the capitals are shown in both front and side elevation. The cornice blocks bear the initials 'CT' (Charles Till, the Clerk of Works), and were designed later. (vol I.63, 26 Aug 1876, 30 Jun 1877. 26.5 x 37.5 cm)

63

48 Four of the series of animals to be made in iron for the cresting of the main roof, carefully identified as the glossy ibis (*Ibis falcinellus*), the white eyelid monkey (*Cercocebus fulginosus*), the common genet (*Genetta vulgaris*) and the crow (*Corvus corone*). There are a total of eight creatures, see also plate 49. (vol II.20, 27 x 36.5 cm)

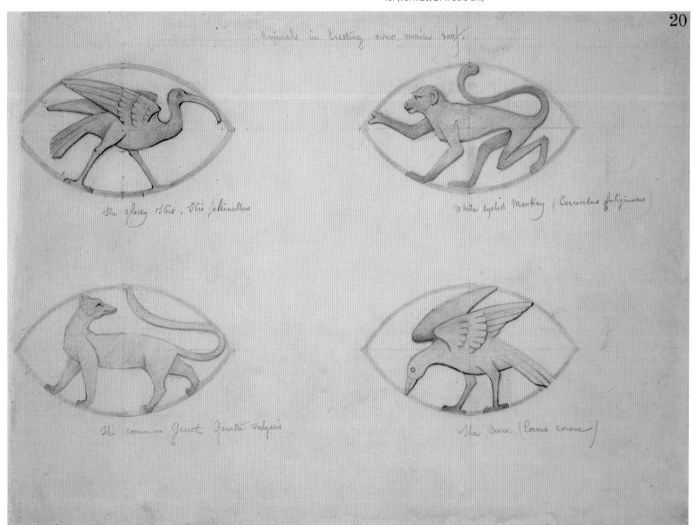

49 Animals to be made in iron for the cresting of the main roof, carefully identified as the kinkajou (*Cercoleptes candivolvulus*), the pterodactyl, the kestrel (*Falco tinnunculus*) and the ring dove (*Columba palumbus*). (vol II.22. 27 x 37 cm)

118

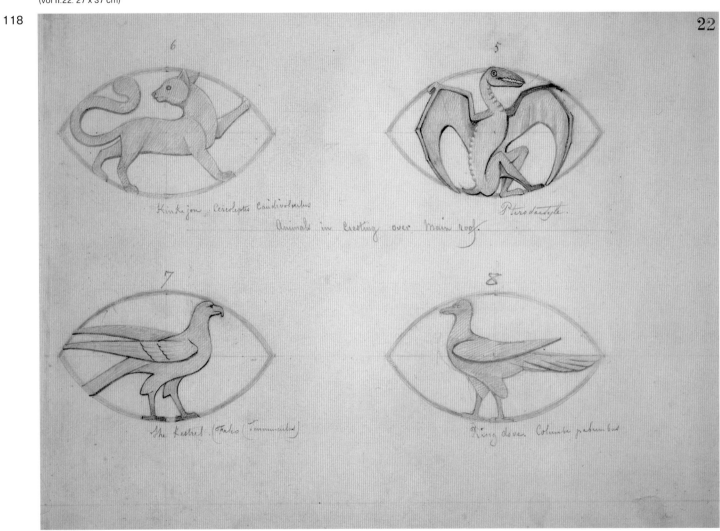

50 Two of the animals, wolf and lion, for the windows of the first floor of the west wing. They form part of a set of three different species that are repeated along the wing. (vol I.19, 26 Feb 1875. 27 x 37 cm)

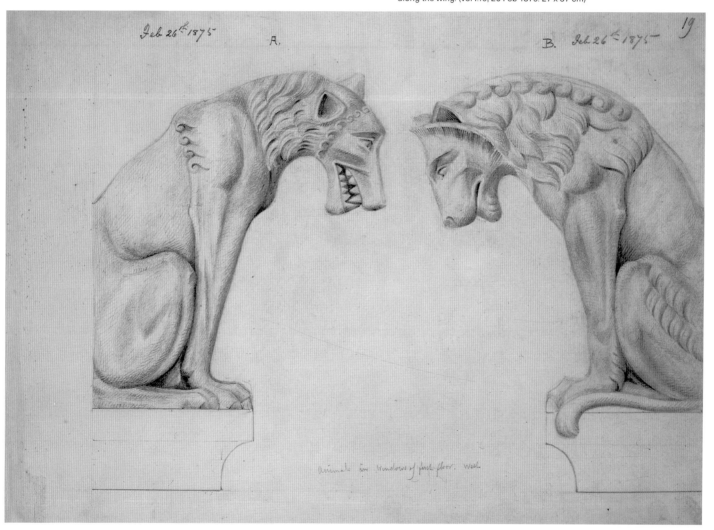

51   Two further animals for the first-floor windows: on the right the hyena for
the west wing and on the left an unidentified extinct mammal for the east wing
(vol I.20, 26 Feb & 16 Mar 1875. 26.5 x 37.5 cm)

120

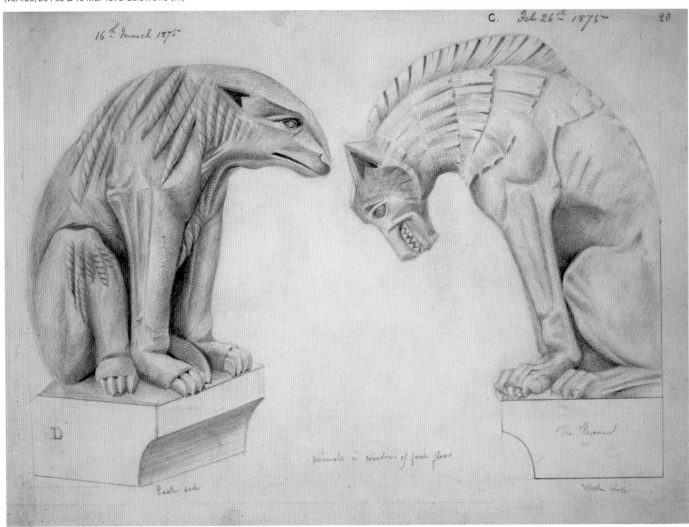

52 Two more extinct animals for the first-floor windows of the east wing. Neither is identified, but they are recognisable as the pterodactyl and the sabre-toothed tiger. (vol I.21, 16 Mar 1875. 26.5 x 37.5 cm)

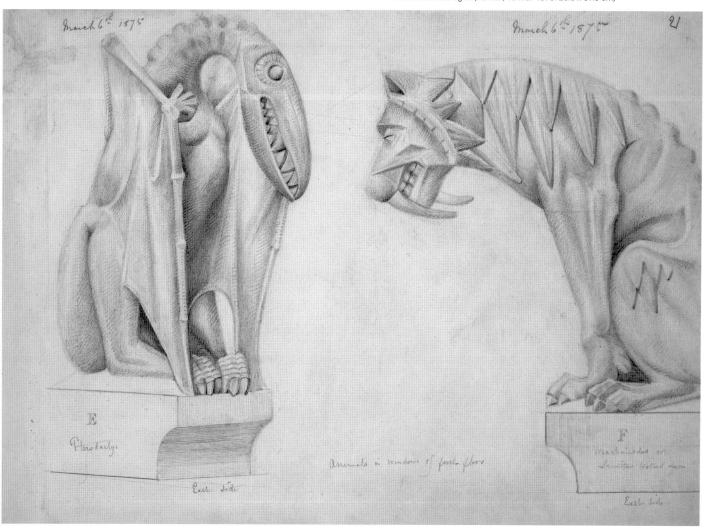

53 Two panels of extinct fish to go beneath the first-floor windows of the
east wing. Once again these are part of a set of four designs. These two formed
a pair, which is repeated alternating with further pairs of the designs in plate
54. The two species are identified as *Osteolepis* and *Dipterus macrotepidotus*
(vol I.22, 26 Feb 1875. 26.5 x 37.5 cm)

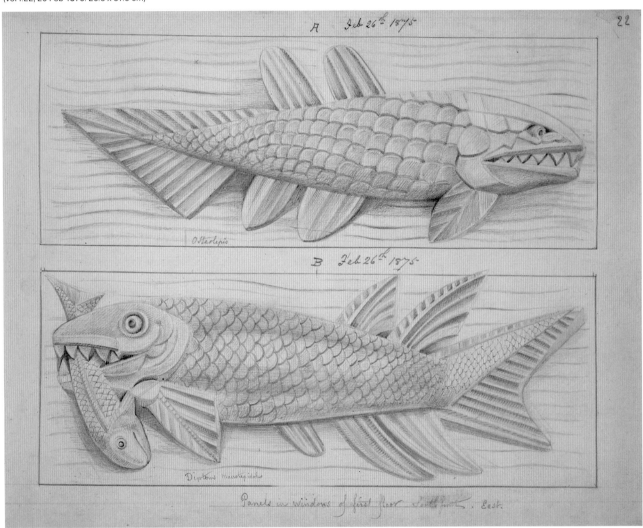

54 Two further panels for the first-floor windows of the east wing showing unidentified foliage and a pair of *Amblirhyncus cristalus* lizards. Each of these was repeated to make a pair under the two lights of a window, and formed part of the triple rhythm with the fish in plate 53. (vol I.23, 6 & 16 Mar 1875. 26.5 x 37.5 cm)

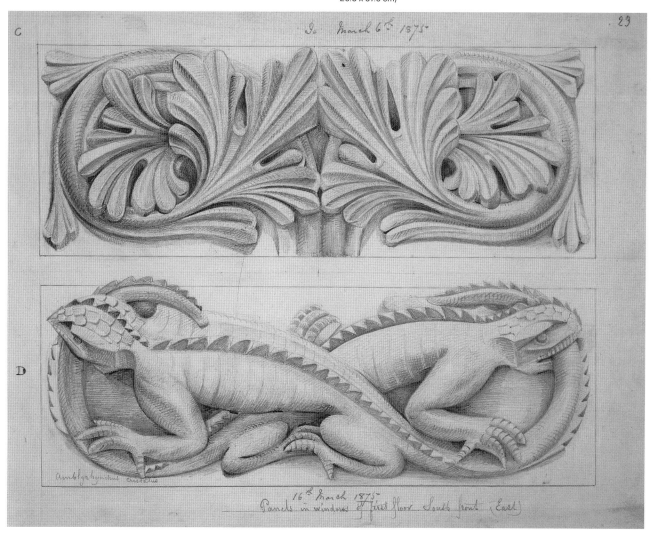

55 Two panels to be set beneath the first-floor windows of the west wing showing foliage and an eel, neither of which is identified. The foliage was repeated to fill the space beneath one window, while the eel was paired with the conger in plate 56. (vol I.24, 26 Feb 1875. 26.5 x 37.5 cm)

124

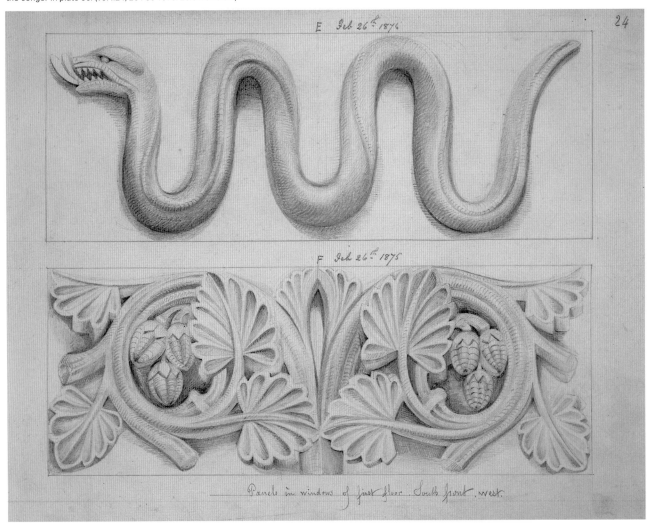

24

E Feb 26th 1875

F Feb 26th 1875

Panels in windows of first floor. South front. west.

56 Two further panels to be set beneath the first-floor windows of the west wing show a *Conger vulgaris* and a pair of stomias, the latter being repeated as a pair under each window where it occurs. (vol I.25, 26 Feb 1875. 26.5 x 37.5 cm)

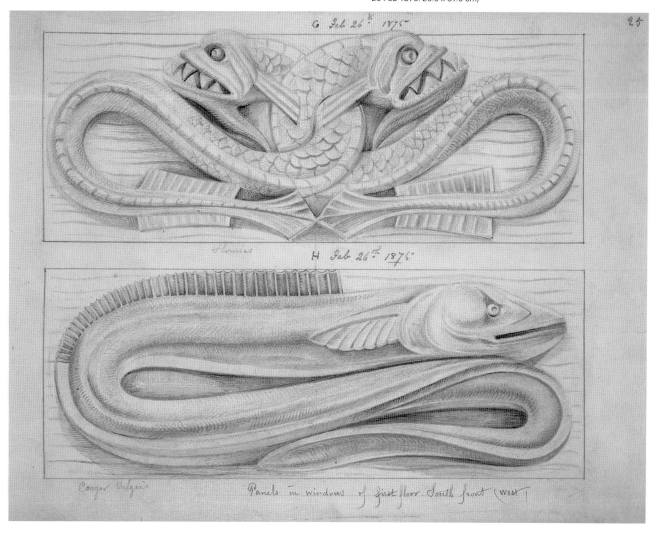

57 A pair of capitals for mullions in the first-floor windows of the south galleries of the east wing show an extinct form of wolf and unidentified foliage. (vol I.16, 24 Feb 1875. 26.5 x 37.5 cm)

58 Design for a triple capital for the right-hand side of the recessed arches in the first-floor windows of the south galleries of the east wing. The left-hand are noted as to be the same. Though dated to January, a note indicates: 'these three caps are not yet finished Feby 1st 1875'. The two labelled C5 & C6 are slightly more firmly drawn and might be by a different hand. (vol I.17, 25 Jan 1875. 26.5 x 37.5 cm)

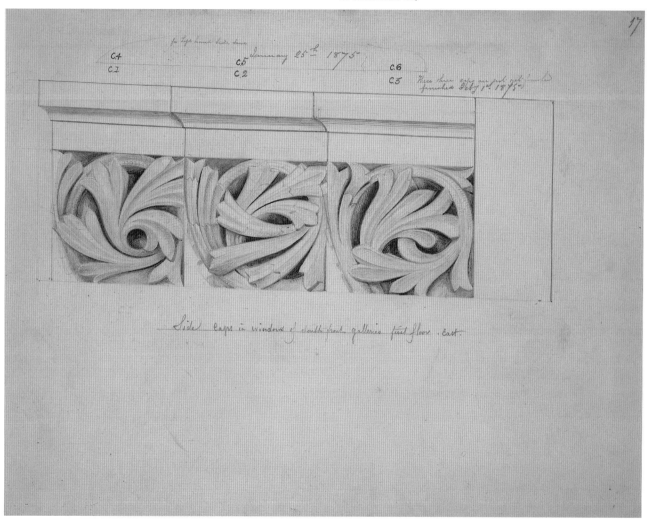

59 A lion and a foliage capital for the mullions in the first-floor windows of the south galleries of the west wing. The perspective of the foliage capital is incorrect, which may explain why it was despatched later. (vol I.15, 25 Jan & 24 Feb 1875. 26.5 x 37.5 cm)

128

60 Design for a triple capital for the right-hand side of the recessed arches in the first-floor windows of the south galleries of the west wing. The double numbering of each capital indicates a reverse version for the other side of each window. 'Six caps' are specified, presumably for each window, since the wings are of eleven bays. A row of leaf enrichment for the first floor of the south galleries was added to the sheet on 3 September 1875. (vol I.18 & 25 Jan 1875. 26.5 x 37.5 cm)

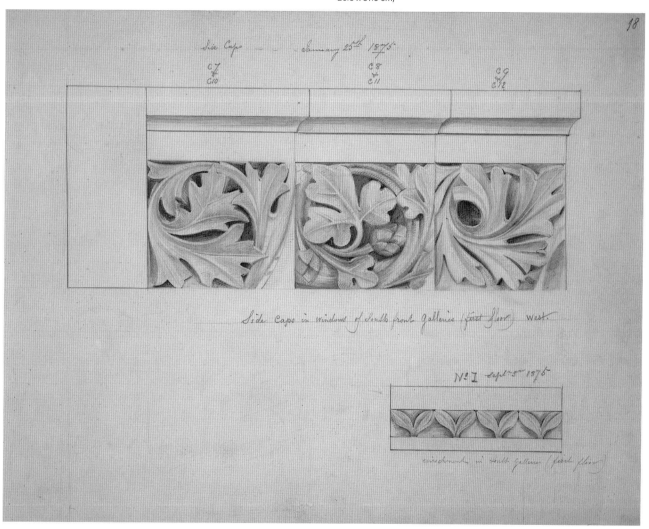

61 Details for the principal entrance. Six different designs for foliage annulets to the shafts, labelled D–I, and four designs for their bases, labelled A–D, which include a beak head and ram's head. (vol I.26, 1 & 6 July 1875. 26.5 x 37.5 cm)

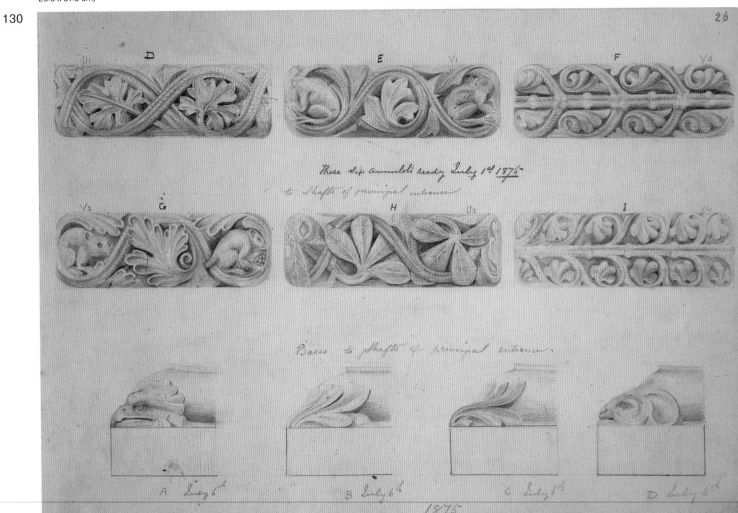

62 Two boldly designed capitals (B & A) from the principal entrance: 'one of the middle caps or 2nd cap from outside on the right going in' and 'outer cap on right hand side of principal entrance doorway'. (vol I.31, 22 Jul 1875. 26.5 x 37.5 cm)

63 A further pair of capitals (D & C) for the entrance. Again, one is designed with a flat rear surface and is the 'inner cap on right hand side going towards the entrance hall', while the other is 'one of the middle caps or second cap from door on right hand side'. The foliage is unidentified. (vol I.30, 22 Jul 1875. 26.5 x 37.5 cm)

132

64 Capitals E & F for the principal entrance, the 'outer cap on left hand side' and 'one of the middle caps or 2nd cap on left hand side going in'. (vol I.33A, 22 Jul 1875. 26.5 x 37.5 cm)

33 A.

133

E F

Outer Caps on Left Hand
side of principal Entrance
doorway
July 22nd 1875

One of the middle caps
or 2nd cap on Left hand
side going in
July 22nd 1875

65 A particularly fine drawing of two capitals (G & H) for the principal
entrance, with details of the necking and the top of the shaft. These are
specially identified as: 'one of the middle caps or 2nd cap from doors coming
out' and 'inner caps next doors on left hand side going into entrance hall', which
explains why its right-hand side is designed flat to lie against the wall. (vol I.29,
22 Jul 1875. 26.5 x 37.5 cm)

134

66 Four foliage capitals for the minor shafts of the principal entrance. They form part of a series of twelve, numbered A to L, of which the remaining eight are shown in plates 62–65. The plants are unidentified, but carefully distinguished. (vol I.28, 1 Jul 1875. 26.5 x 38 cm)

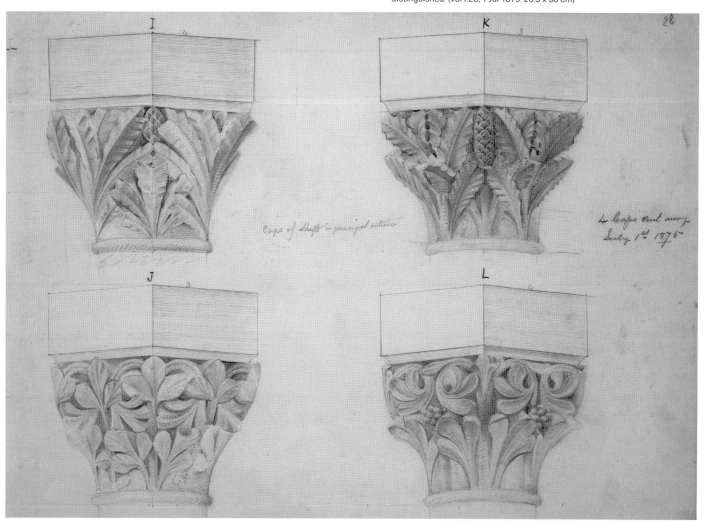

Caps of shafts in principal entrance

4 caps sent away
July 1st 1875

67 Three elevations of a composite capital over the doorway of the principal entrance with birds and a small rodents in foliage, together with capitals for the dormer-window shafts in the south west gallery (A) and south east gallery (B), and a simple shaft base presumably for the same windows. (vol I.41, 7 Oct 1875, 20 Jan & 12 May 1876. 26.5 x 37.5 cm)

136

68 Two elevations of a composite side capital over the doorway of the principal entrance have storks and canines in their foliage. Also a set of pieces for the side balustrade of the first floor of the Index Museum, with two bases and two capitals, labelled A & B, and six different shafts, labelled C to H. The simple patera was designed for the exterior of the east galleries. (vol I.40, 7 & 29 Oct, 21 Dec 1875, 20 Jan, 7, 9 & 17 Feb 1876. 26.5 x 37.5 cm)

69 A larger sheet showing the whole frieze over the principal entrance at a scale of 1 1/2 inches to 1 foot, with goats, foxes, a dog and cat chasing birds in foliage. (vol I.43, 21 Dec 1875. 27 x 72.5 cm)

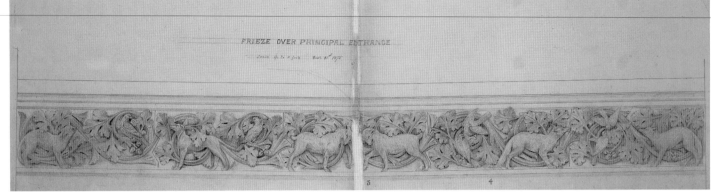

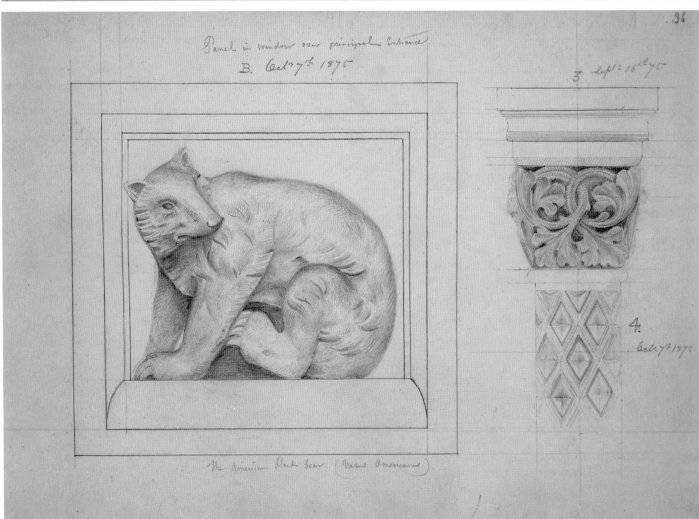

70 The American black bear (*Ursus americanus*) from the set of five panels over the entrance door, and another design for a shaft in the window above. All three pieces were sent at different dates. (vol I.36, 3 Sept, 4 & 7 Oct 1875. 26.5 x 37.5 cm)

71 The great kangaroo (*Macropus major*) panel from the principal entrance, and a capital with three lions heads for the shaft in the window over it. (vol I.37, 4 Sept 1875 & 7 Oct 1875. 26.5 x 37.5 cm)

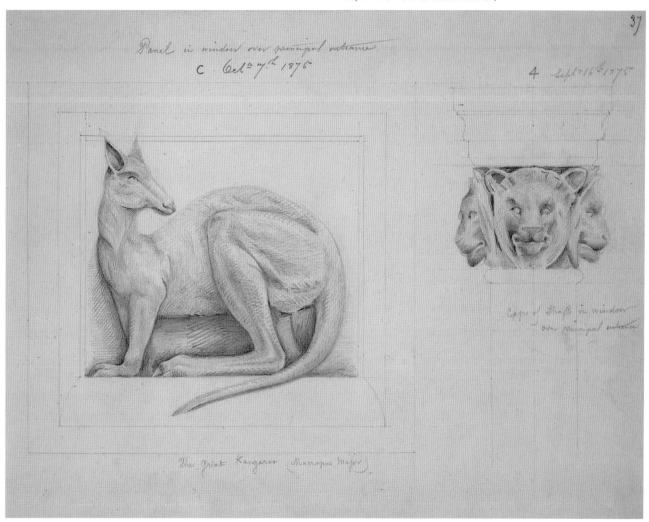

Panel in window over principal entrance
c - Oct.ᵗ 7ᵗʰ 1875

4 Sept 16ᵗʰ 1875

The Great Kangaroo (Macropus Major)

Caps of Shafts in window
over principal entrance

72 The jaguar (*Felis onca*) panel from the principal entrance, and a foliage
capital for a shaft on the window over it. (vol I.38, 7 & 29 Oct 1875.
26.5 x 37.5 cm)

140

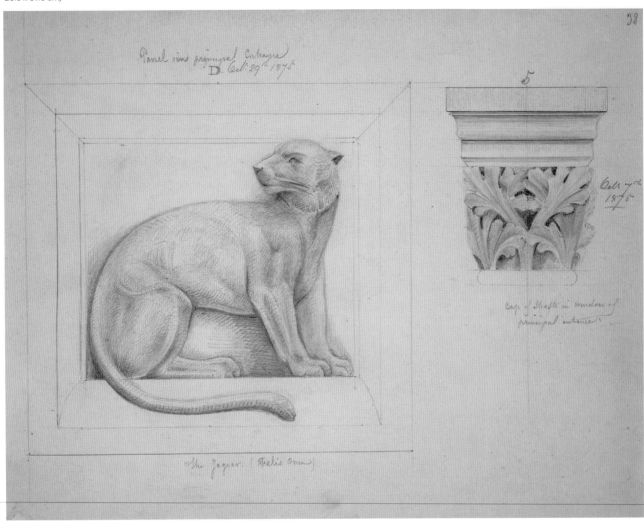

73 A particularly finely finished drawing of the spotted hyena (*Hyena crocuta*) panel for the frieze over the principal entrance (vol I.39, 10 Nov 1875. 26.5 x 37.5 cm)

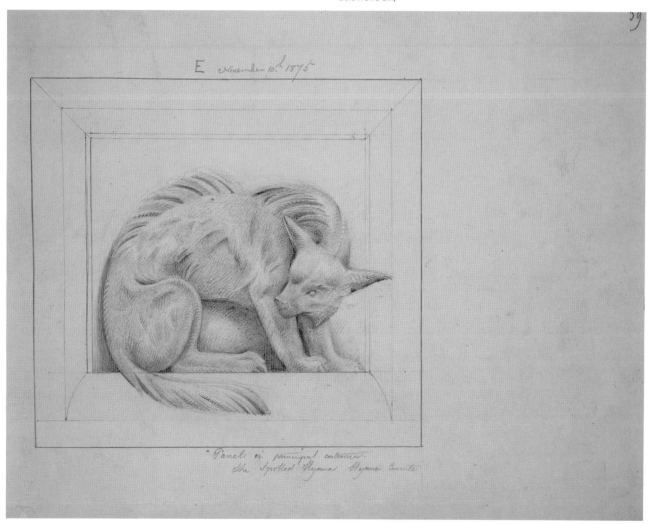

74 Design of a lioness struggling with a snake for the central panel over the principal entrance. Also a shaft for the window over the principal entrance. Base capital and pillar are numbered 1–3 and were sent on different dates. (vol I.34 14 & 16 Sept, 7 Oct 1875. 26.5 x 37.5 cm)

142

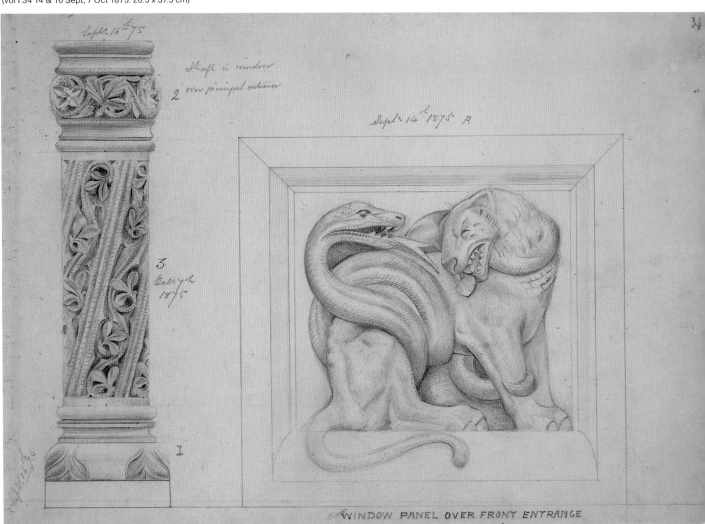

WINDOW PANEL OVER FRONT ENTRANCE

75 Two delightful heads fill the spandrels of the window over the main entrance. They represent a monkey for evolution and a bulldog (*Canis anglicus*) for Britain. (vol I.35, 16 Sept 1875. 26.5 x 37.5 cm)

76 Three elevations of the triple capital in the Entrance Hall showing a fox and cat hunting birds, together with a detail of the annulet for the shafts. The poses of the fox and cat in the front elevation differ from those shown in the side elevations. (vol I.33, 22 Jul 1875. 26.5 x 37.5 cm)

33

77 Perhaps the liveliest of all Waterhouse's designs are the four spandrel pieces that are repeated as springers for the vaults in the bays of the Entrance Hall. These are identified as 'the Iguana', 'the Delundung (*Pisnodon gracilis*)', 'the Racoon' and 'the Seychelles Gecko (*Platydactylus gecko*)'. (vol I.32, 22 Jun 1875. 26.5 x 37.5 cm)

145

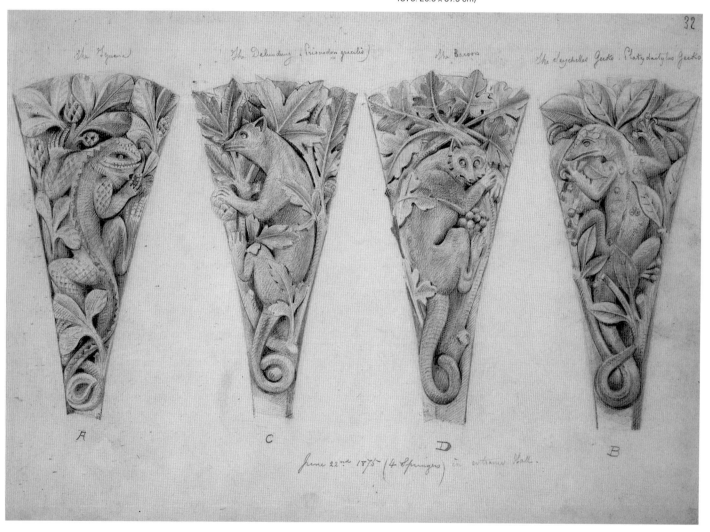

78 A single floret panel. It is not identified, but was used for the pierced terracotta panels in the ventilation grilles on the first floor of the Entrance Hall. (vol II.34., 26.5 x 37.5 cm)

146

79 Two designs for pierced ventilation panels in plaster for the ceilings of the second floor over the Entrance Hall. (vol II.18, 13 Apr 1878. 27 x 37.5 cm)

18

Ventilating panels 2nd floor over Entrance Hall   apl 13/78

80 One of a pair of large roundels for the first floor of the Entrance Hall has a pair of herons (*Ardea cinerea*), one of which is devouring a lizard. (vol I.61, 1 Sept 1876, 26.5 x 37.5 cm).

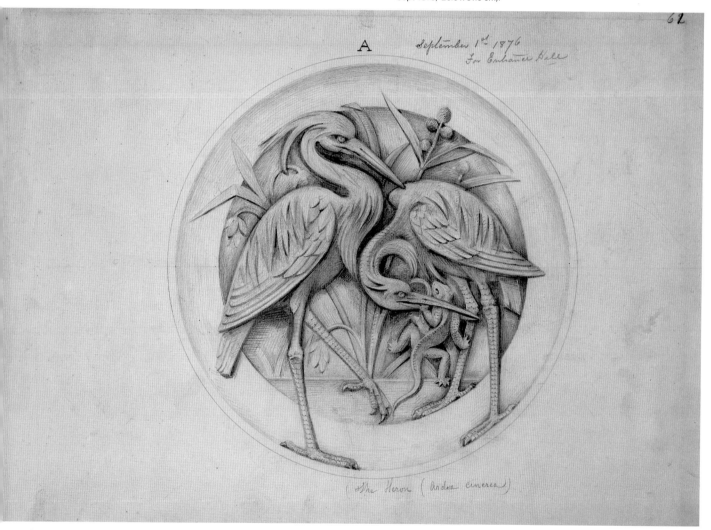

A   September 1st 1876
For Entrance Hall

The Heron (Ardea cinerea)

81   The matching roundel in the Entrance Hall shows an Ibex (*Capra ibex*).
(vol I.62, 12 Oct 1876. 26.5 x 37.5 cm)

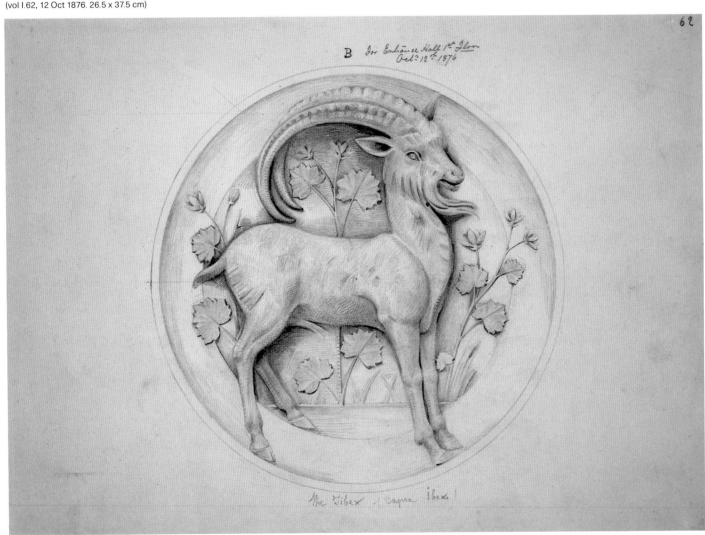

82 Four different designs for capitals, listed A* to D*, and shafts, listed E to H, for the first-floor level. One capital is marked as for the first floor of the Index Museum; all four, however, are labelled for the Entrance Hall. The shafts appear to have been sent for modelling at a later date. A note instructs the builders to 'use most of the two shafts E & F'. (vol I.42, 9 & 17 Feb, 2 & 14 Mar 1876. 27 x 37.5 cm)

83 Two further capitals for double shafts on the first floor of the Index Museum, listed E, F and G, H; and a set of seven blocks of running ornament, labelled A–G, for the soffit of the monkey arches in the Entrance Hall. Blocks A and B alternate for the length of the jambs, while the arches themselves are set with repeating sets of D–G and one further design that does not survive.
(vol I.45, 17 & 30 Mar & 6 April 1876. 26.5 x 37.5 cm)

84 A set of six lively heads for corbels in the Index Museum with the note: 'these six heads sent off to Manufacturers April 7 1876 ready April 16th', an indication of how tight the modelling timetable was. The sheet also contains a design for the capitals in the arcade between the Index Museum galleries and the lobbies of the Refreshment Room, showing the chevron enrichment to the shaft below the joint at the base of the capital. The two springers of the arches, A and B, are also shown. (vol I.47, 7 & 25 Apr 1876. 26.5 x 37.5 cm)

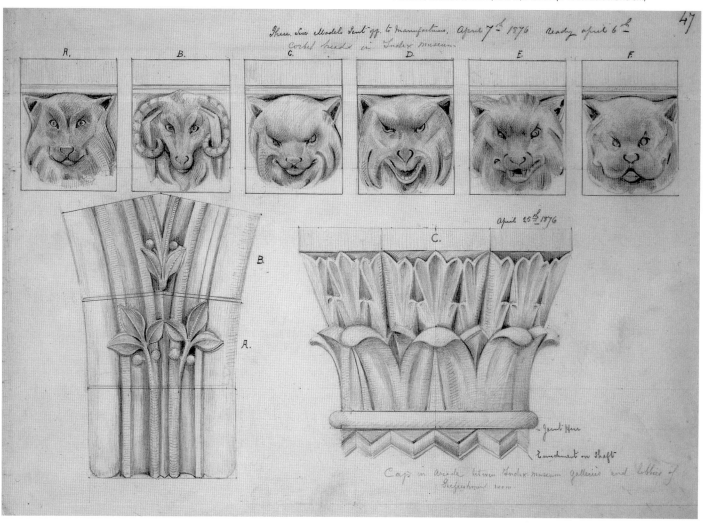

85 A set of voussoirs and a keystone decorated with olive leaves and florets. These were used for the first-floor arcade of the Entrance Hall. The two paterae are labelled for the Refreshment Room, where they were set in the spandrels of the windows. (vol I.46, 12 May 1876. 26.5 x 37.5 cm)

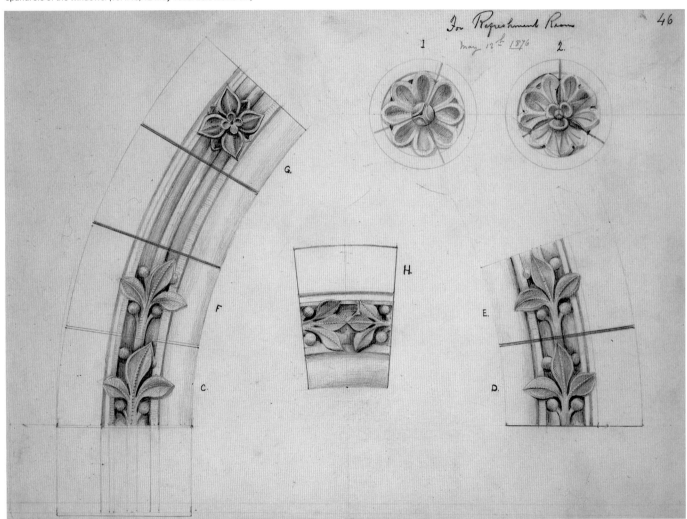

86 A splendid triple capital and a single capital for piers in the Index Museum, together with their bases. These designs are typical of the way in which Waterhouse entwined his animals in foliage, allowing them to be fully visible yet retaining the simple shape of the capital as a whole. (vol I.51, 10 & 13 Jun, 2 Jul 1876. 26.5 x 37.5 cm)

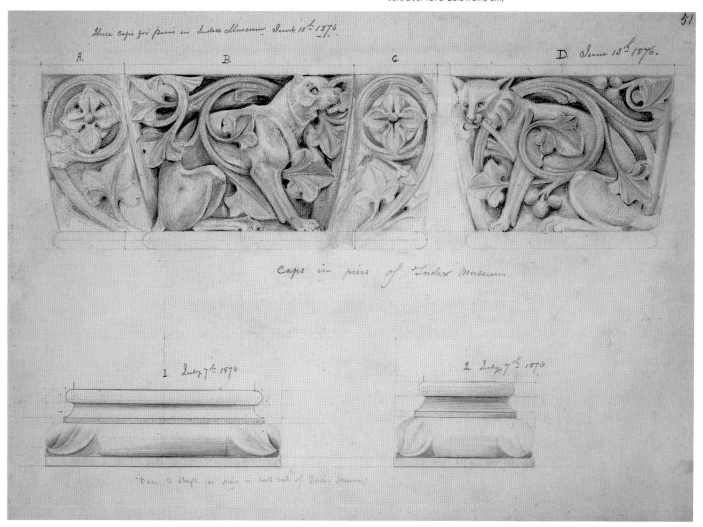

87 Details for the principal staircase and principal entrance. Six large circlets, numbered 1–6, were for the principal entrance, and a base M for the small shafts at the side of the entrance, and N for the cluster of three shafts between the entrance doors. Six smaller circlets, A–F, were for the balustrade of the principal stairs, as were the eight different designs for balusters, numbered 1–8 (with 8 apparently plain), and the three capitals and two bases, A–E. The entrance designs were sent in July and the staircase items not until November (vol I.27, 1 & 2 July, 12 Nov 1875. 26.5 x 37.5 cm)

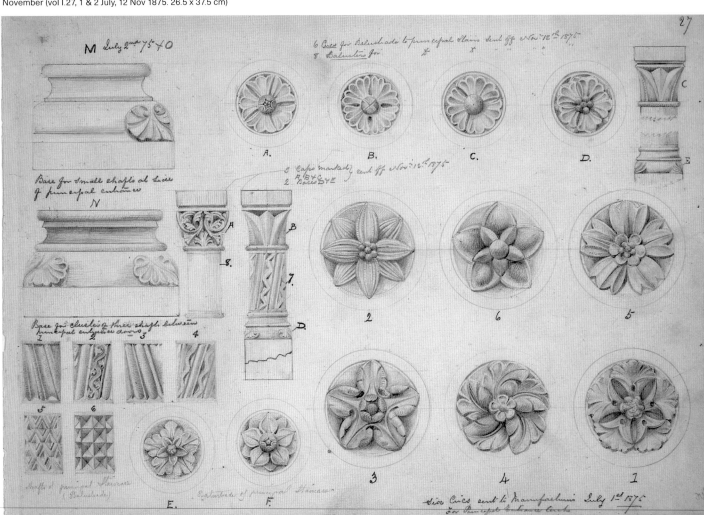

88 Two of the larger panels from the set of fourteen for the principal stair-case, labelled A–N. These two, designed for the ground floor, illustrate the great bustard (*Otis tarda*) and the greyhound, and are signed by the Clerk of Works. (vol II.26, 4 Sept , 30 Oct 1878. 27 x 36 cm)

155

89 Two of the larger panels from the set of fourteen for the ground floor of the principal staircase illustrate the demoiselle crane (*Scops virgo*) and the ounce (*Felis unca*), initialled by the Clerk of Works. (vol II.27, 30 Oct 1878. 27 x 36 cm)

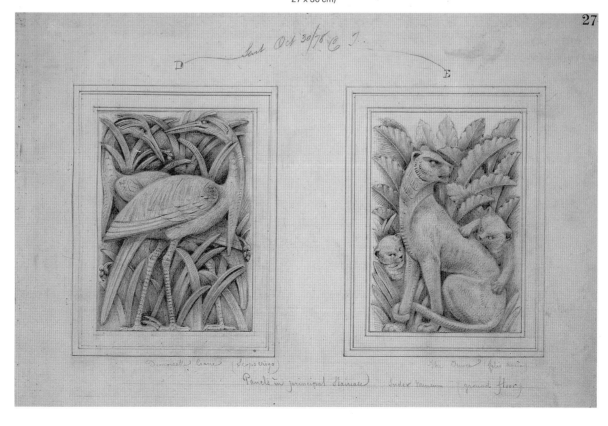

90 Two of the larger panels from the set of fourteen for the ground floor of the principal staircase illustrate the cormorant and the fox (*Vulpes vulgaris*) and are initialled by the Clerk of Works. (vol II.28, 10 & 20 Dec 1878. 27 x 36 cm)

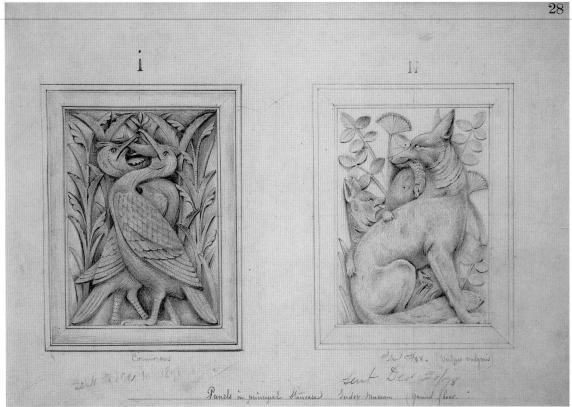

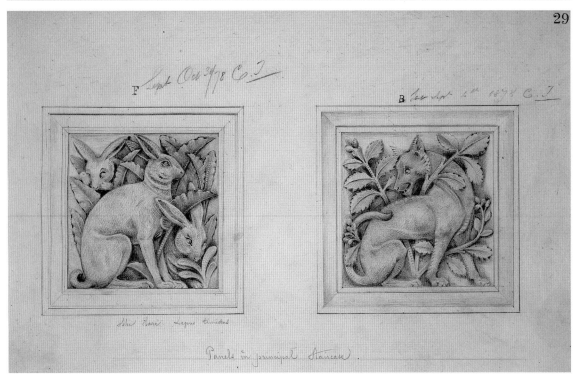

91 Two of the smaller panels from the upper levels of the principal staircase illustrate the hare (*Lepus timidus*) and an unidentified dog; both are initialled by the Clerk of Works. (vol II.29, 4 Sept, 30 Oct 1878. 27 x 37.5 cm)

92 Two of the smaller panels from the upper levels of the principal staircase illustrate wild cats and the golden pheasant (*Thaumalia picta*) and are initialled by the Clerk of Works. (vol II.30, 30 Oct 1878. 27 x 36 cm)

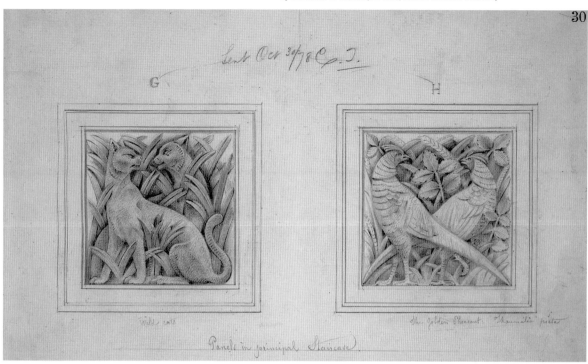

93 Two of the smaller panels from the upper levels of the principal staircase illustrate the cavy (*Cavidae*) and the black grouse (*Tetrao tetrix*). (vol II.31, Dec 1877. 27 x 36 cm)

94 Two of the smaller panels from the upper levels of the principal staircase
illustrate the fennec (*Vulpes zaarensis*) and the palmated stilt plover
(*Cladorhyncus pectoralis*). (vol II.32, 20 Dec 1878. 27 x 36 cm)

95 Designs for the arcade at the north end of the Index Museum include two separate versions of shafts
and capitals with a single base. Two more elaborate capitals were for larger shafts, with a base similar to the
smaller version, together with a cornice block. The note 'for B.N.H.M' shows that these were intended for the
rear hall of the Museum. (vol I.50, 12 & 18 May, 15 June, 12 July 1876. 26.5 x 37.5 cm)

96 A set of eight capitals, lettered A–H, either single or clustered, designed for the blind arcade that decorates the north wall of the Index Museum. The single caps have carefully differentiated foliage and one bird, while the capitals of paired shafts have either a pair of birds, a bear, or the European lynx (*Felis lynx*), the only species of this set that is identified. The entire arcade is fitted with one each of capitals F and H, two of C, three each of A, B, D & E and four of G. (vol I.60, 1 & 9 Aug 1876. 26 x 50.5 cm)

97 Four fierce creatures – two canines, an owl and an eagle – perch astride the gablets that are set against the north wall of the Index Museum. (vol I.59, 11 Jul 1876. 26.5 x 37.5 cm)

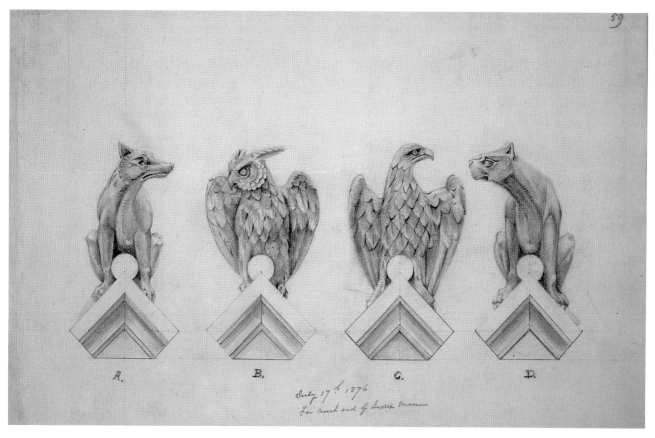

98 One of a pair of roundels for the lobbies to the Refreshment Room on the first floor shows the nandu (*Rhea linnaei*). Uniquely, this is marked as '1/2" scale'. (vol I.65, 12 Oct 1876. 26.5 x 37.5 cm)

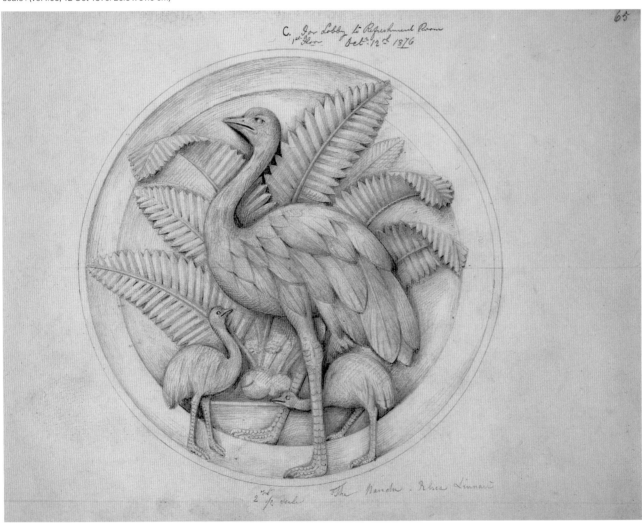

99 The roundel for the south side of the south wall to the Refreshment Room shows the fully identified mazama (*Canepestris guaszuti*) of South America. (vol I.67, 17 Nov 1876. 26.5 x 37.5 cm)

100 A set of fifteen designs for extinct fish, in low relief, for the lower portions of the piers in the ground-floor galleries of the east wing. They are all carefully identified, and the four right-hand blocks also show the inscribed wave pattern that forms the background to all the fish and provides a texture on the blank blocks. This page shows the two ends and the side of a pier. (vol I.9. undated. 26.5 x 37.5 cm)

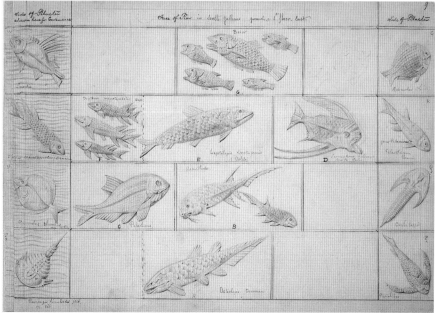

101 A set of nine further designs for fish in low relief, continuing the series in plate 99. Again, the species are identified, and the whole series, on this and the preceding sheet, lettered A–W. (vol I.10, undated. 26.5 x 37.5 cm)

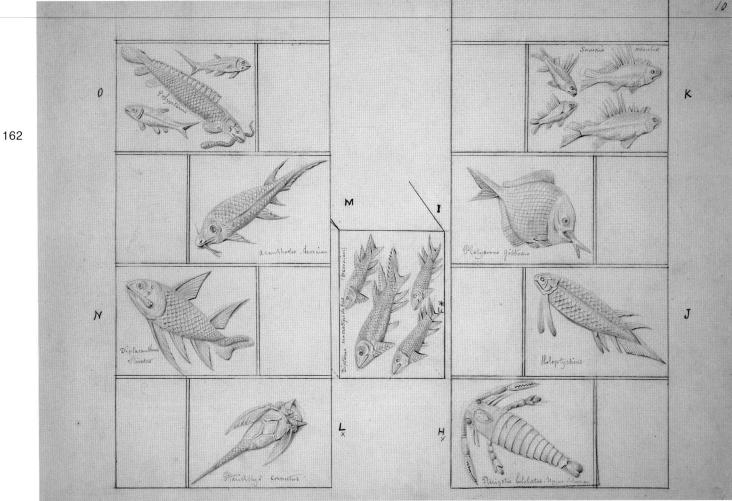

102 Two panels of fossil foliage for the pilasters of the east ground-floor galleries, labelled I and L and with the number 16, presumably the amount required from the manufacturers. (vol I.12, 1 Apr 1875. 26.5 x 37.5 cm)

103 Continuation of the set of panels of fossil foliage for the pilasters of the east ground-floor galleries, labelled G, H, J, and K. A note records that 'these three panels (apparently G, H and I on plate 102) were finished & sent to Builders', presumably from the terracotta manufacturers. Numbers indicate that 9 casts of pieces H and K were ordered and 16 of each of the rest. (vol I.13, 1 Apr 1875. 38 x 26.5 cm)

163

104 Pair of foliage panels from the set of twelve, for the east wing of the
south galleries, first floor, labelled 'Extincts'. Signed 'CT'. (vol II.3, 12 Nov 1877,
12 Jan 1878. 37 x 27 cm)

164

105 Pair of foliage panels from the set of twelve, for the east wing of the south galleries, first floor, identified as I 3 – *Eumopleris artemiseia* and J 4 – *Libocedrus salicorioides*. (vol II.4, 12 Jan 1877. 37 x 27 cm)

165

106 Pair of foliage panels from the set of twelve, for the east wing of the south galleries, first floor, identified as K 5 – *Sphenopleris crenata* and L 6 – *Pachypteris lanceolata*. Initialled by the Clerk of Works. (vol II.5, 12 & 15 Jan 1878. 37 x 27 cm)

166

107 Ram's-head capital for the ground and first floors of the south west galleries, and two versions of bas-relief panels of pomegranate identified as *Punica granatum*, Linn[aeus], for the floral panels that decorate the top of each pier. (vol I.5, 9 May [1875]. 38 x 26.5 cm)

108 Four more versions of the pomegranate panels, also identified, for the piers of the ground-floor galleries. The piers are set in pairs, each having three decorated faces, requiring six casts of each design per pier. Waterhouse was careful to ensure variety by making each panel slightly different. (vol I.6, undated. 38 x 26.5 cm)

168

109 Three versions of a design of *Anona palustris* for the panels in the pilasters of the west ground-floor galleries. The three designs, D, E and F complete the sequence for the west gallery on the ground floor. (vol I.14, 21 Jan 1875. 26.5 x 37.5 cm)

110 Pair of foliage panels from the set of twelve, for the west wing of the south galleries, first floor, identified as A – myristica and B – mandarin orange, and initialled by the Clerk of Works. (vol II.1A, 11 Sept, 15 Oct 1877. 37 x 27 cm)

170

111 Pair of foliage panels, C and D, from a series of twelve, labelled A to L, for the first-floor south galleries in the west wing, decorated with carefully identified living plants and animals; C, parrots and vine; and D, lerot (*Myoxus nitula*) and cherries. Signed by C Till, Clerk of Works. (vol II.1, 12 Nov 1877. 37 x 27 cm)

112 Pair of foliage and animal panels from the set of twelve, for the west wing of the south galleries, first floor, identified as E, chameleon (*Chameleon vulgaris*); the parrot and plant are unidentified; and F, *Coreopsis lanceolata*. Signed 'CT'. (vol II.2, 12 Nov 1877. 37 x 27 cm)

172

113 Two unusual capitals for pilasters in the south east galleries, A and B, labelled 'sent away July 28/77 CT', feature creatures peering out from foliage. The horse and deer are presumably extinct species. (vol I.76, 28 Jul 1877. 26.5 x 38 cm)

Caps of Pilasters in South galleries. (East.)

A

B

Sent away July 28/77 CT

114 Two capitals for pilasters in the south galleries, C and D. The latter is labelled 'east', but both are used in the 'extinct' galleries. These are part of a series labelled A–X, though not all the drawings survive. (vol I.75, 9 May 1877. 26.5 x 37.5 cm)

174

115 A pair of capitals, E and F, for the pilasters of the south east galleries. The bats and plants are unidentified, but are presumably extinct species. (vol II.6, 12 Jan 1878. 27 x 37 cm)

116 A further pair of the animal capitals, I and J, this time for pilasters in the west galleries, with a native pony and a dog peering through leaves. (vol I.77, 9 May 1877. 26.5 x 37.5 cm)

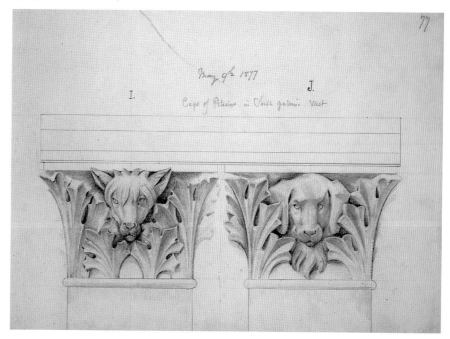

117 Two foliage capitals, K and L, from the south west galleries, with carefully distinguished foliage, fruit and flowers. They are initialled by the Clerk of Works. (vol I.78, 28 Jul 1877. 26.5 x 37.5 cm)

118 Two more of the capitals for pilasters in the galleries of the west wing, M and N, with a cow and what appears to be a mule peering through foliage. (vol I.81, 28 Jul 1877. 26.5 x 37.5 cm)

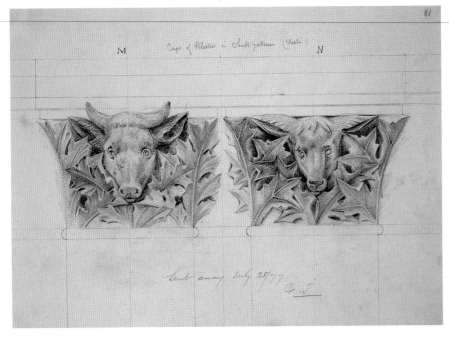

119 Two further capitals, O and P, for the south west galleries with foliage and fruit. The capitals are initialled by the Clerk of Works, and there is a further note: 'and weathering of Smoke Tower same time', suggesting that the purely architectural terracotta was being individually modelled and handled in the same way as the ornamental pieces. (vol I.82, 15 Oct 1877. 26.5 x 37.5 cm)

120 Two views of the capital R for the ground and first floors of the west wing of the south galleries showing a cat in foliage. The position of the capital means that the cat is effectively looking down on the fish that decorate the lower parts of the piers. All these capitals are fitted on paired piers, and this drawing shows the linking abacus with its chevron ornament. The location is entered twice on this sheet, suggesting that more than one draughtsman handled it, though the drawing is clearly autograph Waterhouse. (vol II.7, 20 Nov 1877. 27 x 37.5 cm)

121 Pair of capitals, S, for the west wing of the south galleries, ground and first floor. That on the left shows a wolf's head (*Canis lupus*) and an unidentified head to the side; that on the right shows the brown bear's head (*Ursus arctos*) and a side view of a boar's head (*Sus scrofa*). The sheet bears the signature of the Clerk of Works, C Till. (vol II. 10 & 24 April 1878. 27 x 37.5 cm)

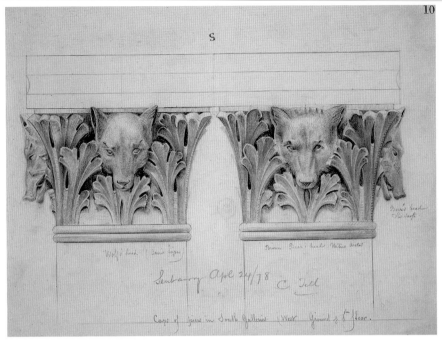

122 Pair of capitals, T, for the west wing of the south galleries, ground and first floor, showing the barn owl (*Strix flammea*) and the great owl (*Bubo maximus*), and signed by the Clerk of Works. (vol II.13, 17 Jul 1878. 27 x 37.5 cm)

123 Pair of capitals, U, for the east wing of the south galleries on ground and first floor showing the outline of the linking abacus. The fossils are separately identified as *Amonites capricornus* and *Criocerus rizoceanus*. Initialled by the Clerk of Works. (vol II.8, 7 Feb 1878. 27 x 37 cm)

179

124 Pair of capitals, V, for the east wing of the south galleries on ground and first floor showing the outline of the linking abacus. The head on the left-hand capital is identified as that of the Palaeotherium, but the side elevation is not identified. The right-hand capital bears the head of *Anoplotherium vulgaris* and, on the side, *Xiphodon gracile*. The sheet bears the signature of the Clerk of Works, C Till. (vol II.9, 11 March 1878. 27 x 37 cm)

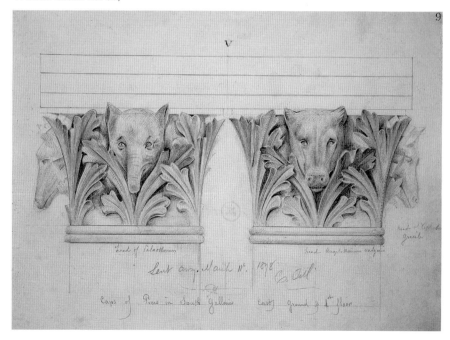

125 Pair of capitals, W, for the east wing of the south galleries, ground and first floor, showing the outline of the linking abacus and initialled by the Clerk of Works. (vol II.11, 18 May 1878. 27.5 x 37.5 cm)

126 Pair of capitals, X, unlabelled, but used for the east wing of the south galleries, ground and first floor, with coralline foliage and showing the outline of the linking abacus, signed by the Clerk of Works. (vol II.12, 1 June 1878. 27 x 37.5 cm)

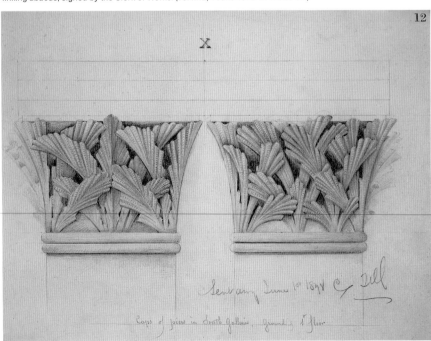

127 One of a pair of lunettes over the doorway in the first-floor south galleries, in this case in the east wing, illustrates the dodo (*Didus ineptus*). (vol II.51. 27 x 37 cm)

128 Set of twelve different corbel blocks with five canines, one shell and six types of foliage. Two panels of foliage for the east and west pavilions respectively. These form the tops of the panels in plate 129 and are drawn across the join of the sketchbook page. (vol I.7, undated. 26.5 x 38 cm)

129 Two panels for the pilasters in the east and west pavilions, showing how Waterhouse enriched the simple foliage stem with a geometric and a serpentine pattern. Neither plant is identified, though the pomegranate is easily recognised. (vol I.8, 5 Jan 1875. 38 x 26.5 cm)

182

130 Half elevations showing the sides of the capitals for the pilasters between the south galleries and the pavilions. A and B are listed as for the east galleries, and D and C for the west, and the sheet is initialled by the Clerk of Works. (vol II.25, 7 Aug 1878. 27 x 37.5 cm)

131 Set of eight floral or shell corbels for the rear galleries of the east wing, together with a design for the base of the shafts in the north galleries and a preliminary and final version of the foliage band for the base of the lamp posts at the principal entrance. These designs were sent to the manufacturers at different dates. (vol I.11, 5 Jan, 28 Apr, 26 Jun 1875. 26.5 x 37.5 cm)

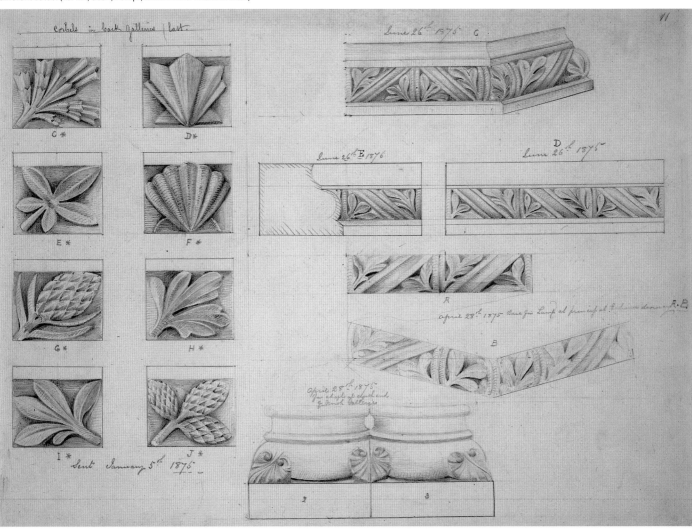

132 A series of minor decorative pieces. A, B, C, A*, B* and C* are voussoirs for the archways between the south galleries and the pavilions on the second floor, together with a keystone and two florets for the archways on the south side of the Entrance Hall on the second floor. A simple capital for the 'balustrade to balconies on the second floor south front and gallery between same'; and four lively heads of a dog, bear and two wolf-like creatures for the corbels of the third floor of the tower. Of these, A, B and C are initialled by Charles Till and were sent on 23 June 1877. (vol I.64, 1 & 25 Sept, 12 Oct 1876, 23 June 1877. 26.5 x 37.5 cm)

64   185

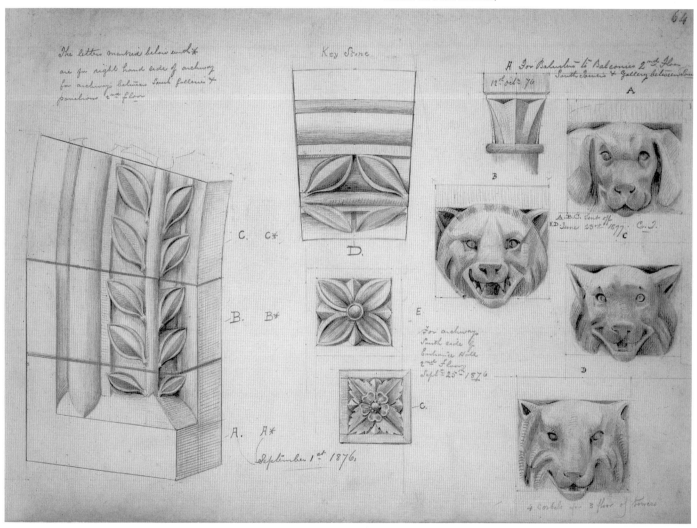

133 A series of five designs for pierced plaster panels to act as ventilators in the back galleries of the ground floor. Each long panel is accompanied by a matching square corner piece (vol II.21. 27 x 37.5 cm)

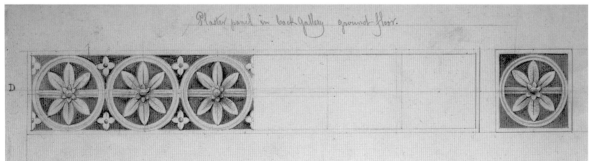

134 Detail showing a sixth pierced plaster panel for the back gallery ground floor. (vol II.24. 27 x 36.5 cm)

135 A roundel with a lion's head for the rear wall of the entrance lodge, a capital for the fourth floor of the pavilions, similar to those for the third floor, and an unidentified floret. All are initialled by the Clerk of Works. (vol I.83, 28 Jun, 4 Sept 1877. 26.5 x 37.5 cm)

187

Appendix

As identified by Waterhouse	Common name	Modern Scientific or Generic name	Plate number(s)	Location(s) in Museum
(names recorded are as spelt by the architect, and may not be as current or 19th century orthography)				

Mammals

As identified by Waterhouse	Common name	Modern Scientific or Generic name	Plate number(s)	Location(s) in Museum
American Black Bear, Ursus Americanus	American black bear	*Ursus americanus*	70	Principal Entrance
Brown Bear, Ursus Arctos	Brown bear	*Ursus arctos*	121	Gallery capital (west)
Boar	Wild boar	*Sus scrofa*	121	Gallery capital (west)
Bulldog, Canis Anglicus	Bulldog	*Canis familiaris*	75	Principal Entrance
Wild Cats	Wildcat	*Felis silvestris*	92	Principal Staircase
Cavy (Cavidae)	Mara	*Dolichotis patagonium*	93	Principal Staircase
Delundung, Prisnodon Gracilis	Banded linsang	*Prionodon linsang*	77	Entrance Hall Springer
Dog, Canis	Dog	*Canis familiaris*	24	Gable Roundel (west)
Fennec, Vulpes Zaarensis	Fennec fox	*Vulpes zerda*	94	Principal Staircase
Fox, Vulpes Vulgaris	Red fox	*Vulpes vulpes*	26, 90	Gable Roundel (west), Principal Staircase
Galago Senegalensis	Senegal bushbaby	*Galago senegalensis*	9	Gate Pier
Genet, Genetta Vulgaris	Common genet	*Genetta genetta*	48	Roof cresting
Goat, Caper Hiscus	Wild goat	*Capra hircus aegagrus*	25	Gable Roundel (west)
Greyhound	Greyhound	*Canis familiaris*	88	Principal Staircase
Hare, Lepus Timidus	Brown hare/European hare	*Lepus europaeus*	91	Principal Staircase
Hyaena	Striped hyena	*Hyaena hyaena*	51	First Floor Windows (west)
Hyaena (spotted), Hyaena Crocuta	Spotted hyena	*Crocuta crocuta*	73	Principal Entrance
Ibex, Capra Ibex	Ibex	*Capra ibex*	81	Roundel, Entrance Hall, first floor
Jaguar, Felis Onca	Jaguar	*Panthera onca*	72	Principal Entrance
Kangaroo (great), Macropus Major	Eastern grey kangaroo	*Macropus giganteus*	71	Principal Entrance
Kinkajou, Cercolpetes Candivolvulus	Kinkajou	*Potos flavus*	49	Roof Cresting
Lerot, Myoxus Nitela	Garden doormouse	*Eliomys quercinus*	111	Gallery Piers, first floor (west)
Lion	Lion	*Panthera leo*	36	Parapet (west)
Lion, Scimitar-toothed	-	-	38, 52	Parapet (east), First Floor Windows (east)
Lynx, European, Felis Lynx	Eurasian lynx	*Lynx lynx*	96	Index Museum, north wall)
Mazama Canepestris Guaszuti	Pampas deer	*Ozotoceros bezoarticus*	99	Roundel, Index Museum, first floor
Monkey	Old World monkey	*Cercopithecidae*	75	Principal Entrance
Monkey, White Eyelid, Cercocebus Fulginosus	White-collared mangabey	*Cercocebus torquatus*	48	Roof Cresting
Ounce, Felis Uncia	Snow leopard	*Uncia uncia*	89	Principal Staircase
Panther	Leopard	*Panthera pardus*	37	Parapet (west)
Racoon, Procyon Lotor	Common racoon	*Procyon lotor*	77, 96	Entrance Hall Springer, Index Museum: north wall
Rat, Black, Mus Rattus	Black rat	*Rattus rattus*	14	Gate Pier
Sajou, Brown, Cibus Apella	Brown capuchin monkey	*Cebus apella*	7	Gate Pier
Squirrel, Red, Sciurus Vulgaris	Red squirrel	*Sciurus vulgaris*	16	Gate Pier
Weasel, Mustela Vulgaris	Weasel	*Mustela nivalis*	6	Gate Pier
Wolf, Canis Lupas	Wolf	*Canis Lupus*	35, 121	Parapet West, Gallery Capital (west)

Birds

As identified by Waterhouse	Common name	Modern Scientific or Generic name	Plate number(s)	Location(s) in Museum
Bustard, Otis tarda	Great bustard	*Otis tarda*	88	Principal Staircase
Cormorant	Great cormorant	*Phalacrocorax carbo*	90	Principal Staircase
Crane, Demoiselle, Scrops Virgo	Demoiselle crane	*Anthropoides virgo*	89	Principal Staircase
Crow, Corvus Corone	Carrion crow	*Corvus corone*	48	Roof Cresting
Crow, Scaled Fruit, Coracina Scutata	Red-ruffled fruit crow	*Pyroderus scutatus*	15	Gate Pier
Dodo, Didus Ineptus	Dodo	*Raphus cucullatus*	127	Gallery Panel (east)
Dove, Ring, Columba Palumbus	Common wood-pigeon	*Columba palumbus*	49	Roof Cresting
Eagle	Golden eagle	*Aquila chrysaetos*	27	Gable Roundel (east & west)
Grouse, Tetrao Tetrix	Black grouse	*Tetrao tetrix*	93	Principal Staircase
Hen Harrier, Circus Cyaneus	Hen harrier	*Circus cyaneus*	12	Gate Pier
Heron, Ardea Cinerea	Grey heron	*Ardea cinerea*	80	Roundel Entrance Hall
Ibis, Glossy, Ibis Falcinellus	Glossy ibis	*Plegadis falcinellus*	48	Roof Cresting
Kestrel, Falco Tinnunculus	Eurasian Kestral	*Falco tinnunculus*	49	Roof Cresting
Owl, Barn, Strix Flammea	Common barn-owl	*Tyto alba*	122	Gallery Capital (west)
Owl Great, Bubo Maximus	Eurasian eagle-owl	*Bubo bubo*	122, 13	Gallery Capital (west), Gate Pier
Parakeet, Alexandrine, Palaeornis Alexandri	Indian red-breasted parakeet	*Psittacula alexandri*	17	Gate Pier
Parrot	Parrot	*Psittacidae*	111	Gallery Pier, First Floor (west)
Pheasant, Golden, Thaumalia Picta	Golden pheasant	*Chrysolophus pictus*	92	Principal Staircase
Pigeon, Passenger, Ectopistes Migratorius	Passenger pigeon	*Ectopistes migratorius*	10	Gate Pier
Plover, Palmated Stilt, Cladorhyncus Pectoralis	Australian stilt	*Himantopus leucocephalus*	94	Principal Staircase
Rhea Linnaei	Lesser Rhea	*Pterocnemia pennata*	98	Roundel, Index Museum, first floor
Wagtail, Pied, Motacilla Yarellii	White wagtail	*Motacilla alba*	18	Gate Pier
Warbler, Garden, Curruca Hortensis	Orphean warbler	*Sylvia hortensis*	19	Gate Pier

Reptiles & Amphibians

As identified by Waterhouse	Common name	Modern Scientific or Generic name	Plate number(s)	Location(s) in Museum
Amblyrhyncus Cristalus	Marine Iguana	*Amblyrhynchus cristatus*	54	First Floor Windows (east)
Asps	(stylised snakes)		11	Gate Pier
Chameleon	Chameleon	*Chamaeleo chameleon*	112	Gallery Piers, first floor (west)
Cobra, The Haje of Egypt	Cobra	*Naja haje*	5	Gate Pier
Gecko, Seychelles	Day Gecko	*Phelsuma* sp.	77	Entrance Hall Springer
Iguana	Iguana	*Iguana iguana*	77	Entrance Hall Springer
Iguana, Smooth-necked	West Indian Iguana	*Iguana delicatissima*	8	Gate Pier

Fish

As identified by Waterhouse	Common name	Modern Scientific or Generic name	Plate number(s)	Location(s) in Museum
Acanthodes	Acanthodian	*Acanthodes* sp.	100	Gallery Pier (east)
Aechmodus	Ray-finned fish	*Dapedium* sp.	100	Gallery Pier (east)
Berix	Alfonsino	*Beryx* sp.	100	Gallery Pier (east)
Cephalaspis	Jawless fish	*Cephalaspis* sp.	100	Gallery Pier (east)
Conger Vulgaris	Conger eel	*Conger conger*	56	First Floor Windows (west)
Diplocanthus Striatus	Acanthodian	*Diplacanthus striatus*	101	Gallery Pier (east)
Dipterus Macrolepidotus	Lungfish	*Dipterus valenciennesi*	53, 100, 101	First Floor Windows (east), Gallery Pier (east)
Hemiaspis Lumuloides			100	Gallery Pier (east)
Holoptychius	Lobe-finned fish	*Holoptychius* sp.	101	Gallery Pier (east)
Leptolepis Spratheformis	Ray-finned fish	*Leptolepides sprattiformis*	100	Gallery Pier (east)
Osteolepis	Lobe-finned fish	*Osteolepis* sp.	53, 100	First Floor Windows (east), Gallery Pier (east)
Palaeohiscus	Ray-finned fish	*Palaeoniscus freieslebenensis*	100	Gallery Pier (east)
Palaeothrissum		*Palaeoniscus* sp.	100	Gallery Pier (east)
Platysomus Gibbosus	Ray-finned fish	*Platsomus gibbosus*	101	Gallery Pier (east)
Polypterus	Bichir	*Polypterus* sp.	101	Gallery Pier (east)
Pterichthys	Placoderm	*Pterichthyodes milleri*	100	Gallery Pier (east)
Pterichthys Cornutus		*Pterichthyodes milleri*	101	Gallery Pier (east)

Pterigotus Bilobatus	Sea scorpion (not a fish)	*Pterygotus bilobatus*	101	Gallery Pier (east)
Pycnidus Rhombus	Ray-finned fish	*Pycnodus*	100	Gallery Pier (east)
Semaphorus Bellicans			100	Gallery Pier (east)
Smerdis Menitus	Ray-finned fish	*Dapalis minutus*	101	Gallery Pier (east)
Smerotes			100	Gallery Pier (east)
Stomias	Scaly dragonfish	*Stomias* sp.	56	First Floor Windows (west)

Dinosaurs & Fossils

Amonites Capricornus	Ammonite	*Aegoceras capricornus*	123	Gallery Capital (east)
Anoplotherium Vulgaris		*Anoplotherium commune*	124	Gallery Capital (east)
Crioceros Rhizoceanus	Ammonite		123	Gallery Capital (east)
Mylodon	Darwin's ground sloth	*Mylodon darwinii*	39	Parapet (east)
Palaeotherium		*Palaeotherium magnum*	30, 124	Gable Roundel (east), Gallery Capital (east)
Palaeotherium, Great		*Palaeotherium magnum*	40	Parapet (east)
Pterodactyl	Pterosaur		28, 49, 52	Gable Roundel (east), Roof Cresting (east), First Floor Windows (east)
Xiphodon Gracile		*Xiphodon gracilis*	29, 124	Gable Roundel (east), Gallery Capital (east)

Plants

Aconitum Napellus	Monkshood	Ranunculaceae: *Aconitum napellus*		Ceiling Panel, British Museum of Natural History
Aesculus Hippocastanum	Horse chestnut	Hippocastanaceae: *Aesculus hippocastanum*		Ceiling Panel, Entrance Hall
Akesia Africana	Akee	Sapindaceae: *Blighia sapida*		Ceiling Panel, Entrance Hall
Aloe Succotrina	Aloe	Aloeaceae: *Aloe vera*		Ceiling Panel, Entrance Hall
Amygdalus Persica	Almond	Rosaceae: *Prunus dulcis*		Ceiling Panel, Index Museum
Anona Palustris	Custard apple	Annonaceae: *Annona glabra*	109	Gallery Piers, Ground Floor (west)
Banksia Speciosa	Showy banksia	Proteaceae: *Banksia speciosa*		Ceiling Panel, Index Museum
Buten Frondosa	Flame of the forest	Leguminosae: *Butea frondosa*		Ceiling Panel, Entrance Hall
Calotropis Procera	Milkweed (Apple of Sodom)	Asclepiadaceae: *Calotropis procera*		Ceiling Panel, Entrance Hall
Camelia Thea	Tea	Theaceae: *Camellia sinensis*		Ceiling Panel, Entrance Hall
Cassia Fistula	Senna	Leguminosae: *Cassia fistula*		Ceiling Panel, Entrance Hall
Cerasus Communis	Cherry	Rosaceae: *Prunus cerasus*		Ceiling Panel, Entrance Hall
Cherry	Cherry	Rosaceae: *Prunus cerasus*	111	Gallery Piers, First Floor (west)
Citrus Aurantium	Citron	Rutaceae: *Citrus aurantium*		Ceiling Panel, Index Museum
Citrus Bergamea	Bergamot	Rutaceae: *Citrus bergamia*		Ceiling Panel, Entrance Hall
Citrus Limonum	Lemon	Rutaceae: *Citrus limon*		Ceiling Panel, Index Museum
Citrus Medica	Citron	Rutaceae: *Citrus medica*		Ceiling Panel, Entrance Hall
Coffea Arabica	Coffee	Rubiaceae: *Coffea arabica*		Ceiling Panel, Entrance Hall
Coreopsis Lanceolata	Tickseed	Compositae: *Coreopsis lanceolata*	112	Gallery Piers, First Floor (west)
Cornus Capitata	Dogwood	Cornaceae: *Cornus capitata*		Ceiling Panel, Entrance Hall
Corylua Avelana	Hazel	Betulaceae: *Corylus avellana*		Ceiling Panel, British Museum of Natural History
Daphne Laureola	Laurel	Thymeleaceae: *Daphne laureola*		Ceiling Panel, British Museum of Natural History
Datura Stramonum	Thorn apple or Jimson Weed	Solanaceae: *Datura stramonium*		Ceiling Panel, British Museum of Natural History
Digitalis Purpures	Foxglove	Scrophulariaceae: *Digitalis purpurea*		Ceiling Panel, British Museum of Natural History
Dilknia Ornata		Dilleniaceae: *Dillenia indica* ?		Ceiling Panel, Entrance Hall
Diospyros Embryopteris	Persimmon	Ebenaceae: *Diospyros kaki*		Ceiling Panel, Entrance Hall
Eremopleris Artemisien	a Paleozoic seed fern	Eremopteris artemisiaefolia	105	Gallery Piers, First Floor (east)
Eucalyptus Globulus	Blue gum	Myrtaceae: *Eucalyptus globulus*		Ceiling Panel, Index Museum
Euphorbium Angustifolium	Rosebay willowherb	Onagraceae: *Epilobium angustifolium*		Ceiling Panel, British Museum of Natural History
Ficus Carica	Edible fig	Moraceae: *Ficus carica*		Ceiling Panel, Index Museum
Garcinia Hanburii	Mangosteen	Guttiferae: *Garcinia mangostana*		Ceiling Panel, Entrance Hall
Glaceum Leuteum	horned poppy	Papaveraceae: *Glaucium flavum*		Ceiling Panel, British Museum of Natural History
Gorcinia Indica	Goa butter	Guttiferae: *Garcinia indica*		Ceiling Panel, Entrance Hall
Gossypium Barbadense	Cotton	Malvaceae: *Gossypium barbadense*		Ceiling Panel, Entrance Hall
Helleborus Niger	Christmas rose	Ranunculaceae: *Helleborus niger*		Ceiling Panel, British Museum of Natural History
Helleborus Viridis	Green hellebore	Ranunculaceae: *Helleborus viridus*		Ceiling Panel, British Museum of Natural History
Ilex Aquifolium	Holly	Aquifoliaceae: *Ilex aquifolium*		Ceiling Panel, Entrance Hall
Inula Helenum	Elecampane	Compositae: *Inula helenium*		Ceiling Panel, British Museum of Natural History
Libocedrus Salecorioides	a fossil conifer	Libocedrus salicornioides	105	Gallery Piers, First Floor (east)
Lonicera Periclymenum	Honeysuckle	Caprifoliaceae: *Lonicera periclymenum*		Ceiling Panel, British Museum of Natural History
Magnolia Auriculata	Magnolia	Magnoliaceae: *Magnolia fraseri*		Ceiling Panel, Entrance Hall
Malva Sylvestris	Mallow	Malvaceae: *Malva sylvestris*		Ceiling Panel, British Museum of Natural History
Mandarin Orange	Mandarin orange	Rutaceae: *Citrus reticulata*	110	Gallery Piers, First Floor (west)
Melanorrhea Usitata	"Theetsee"	Anacardiaceae: *Gluta usitata*		Ceiling Panel, Entrance Hall
Miristica	Nutmeg	Myristicaceae: *Myristica fragrans*	110	Gallery Piers, First Floor (west)
Myristica Fragrans	Nutmeg	Myristicaceae: *Myristica fragrans*		Ceiling Panel, Entrance Hall
Myroxylon Pereirae	Balsam of Peru	Leguminosae: *Myroxylon balsamum var. pereirae*		Ceiling Panel, Entrance Hall
Nicotiana Tabacum	Tobacco	Solanaceae: *Nicotiana tabacum*		Ceiling Panel, Entrance Hall
Olea Europa	Olive	Oleaceae: *Olea europaea*		Ceiling Panel, Index Museum
Onopordum Acanthum	Scotch thistle	Compositae: *Cirsium vulgare*		Ceiling Panel, British Museum of Natural History
Pachypteris Lanceolata	a Mesozoic seed fern	Pachypteris lanceolata	106	Gallery Piers, First Floor (east)
Pinus Silvestris	Scots pine	Pinaceae: *Pinus sylvestris*		Ceiling Panel, Index Museum
Polygonum Bistorta	Bistort	Polygonaceae: *Polygonum bistorta*		Ceiling Panel, British Museum of Natural History
Prunus Amygdalus	Peach	Rosaceae: *Prunus persica*		Ceiling Panel, Entrance Hall
Prunus Domesticus	Plum	Rosaceae: *Prunus domestica*		Ceiling Panel, Entrance Hall
Punica Granatum	Pomegranate	Punicaceae: *Punica granatum*	107, 108	Gallery Piers, Ground Floor (west), Ceiling Panel, Entrance Hall
Pyrus Communis	Pear	Rosaceae: *Pyrus communis*		Ceiling Panel, Entrance Hall
Pyrus Cydonia	Quince	Rosaceae: *Cydonia oblonga*		Ceiling Panel, Entrance Hall
Pyrus Indica		Rosaceae: *Docynia indica*		Ceiling Panel, Entrance Hall
Pyrus Malus	Apple	Rosaceae: *Malus pumila*		Ceiling Panel, Index Museum
Quassia Amara	Quassia	Simaroubaceae: *Quassia amara*		Ceiling Panel, Entrance Hall
Quercus Robor	Oak	Fagaceae: *Quercus robur*		Ceiling Panel, Index Museum
Quercus Tinctoria	Oak	Fagaceae: *Quercus tinctoria*		Ceiling Panel, Entrance Hall
Ranunculus Lingua	Buttercup	Ranunculaceae: *Ranunculus lingua*		Ceiling Panel, British Museum of Natural History
Ricinus Communis	Castor oil	Euphorbiaceae: *Ricinus communis*		Ceiling Panel, Entrance Hall
Rhododendrum Formosum	Rhododendron	Ericaceae: *Rhododendron formosum*		Ceiling Panel, Entrance Hall
Rosa Canina	Dog rose	Rosaceae: *Rosa canina*		Ceiling Panel, British Museum of Natural History
Saccharum Officinarum	Sugar cane	Gramineae: *Saccharum officinarum*		Ceiling Panel, Entrance Hall
Sambucus Nigra	Elder	Caprifoliaceae: *Sambucus nigra*		Ceiling Panel, British Museum of Natural History
Sonchus palustris	Sow thistle	Compositae: *Sonchus oleraceus*		Ceiling Panel, British Museum of Natural History
Sphenopleris Crenata	a Paleozoic seed fern	Sphenopteris crenata	106	Gallery Piers, First Floor (east)
Strychnos Nux Vomica	Strychnine	Loganiaceae: *Strychnos nux-vomica*		Ceiling Panel, Entrance Hall
Theobroma Cacao	Cocoa	Sterculiaceae: *Theobroma cacao*		Ceiling Panel, Index Museum
Vitis Vinifera	Grape vine	Vitaceae: *Vitis vinifera*		Ceiling Panel, Index Museum
Zea Mays	Sweet corn	Gramineae: *Zea mays*		Ceiling Panel, Entrance Hall

Bibliography

Cunningham, Colin & Prudence Waterhouse, *Alfred Waterhouse 1830–1905: Biography of a Practice,* Oxford University Press (Oxford), 1992

Desmond, Adrian, *Archetypes and Ancestors: Palaeontology in Victorian London, 1850–1875,* Chicago University Press (Chicago), 1984

Desmond, Adrian, *Huxley,* Penguin Books (Harmondsworth), 1998

Desmond, Adrian L Moore, Jim *Darwin* Penguin Books (Harmondsworth) 1992

Dictionary of Art, Macmillan/Grove (London), 1996

Dixon, Henry, *Twelve Photographs of the Natural History Museum of Great Britain from points of view selected by the architect, A. Waterhouse, Esq, ARA* (London), 1881, published by special permission

Girouard, Mark, *Alfred Waterhouse and the Natural History Museum*, The Natural History Museum (London), 1981, reprinted 1999

Gosmani Laszló, *Vocabularium Nominum Animalium Europae Septem Linguis Redactum,* Akademiai Kidokiado (Budapest), 1979

Gould, Stephen Jay, 'Knight Takes Bishop?', *Natural History 95 (5)*, 1986, pp18–33

Ingles, Jean M & Frederick C Sawyer, 'A Catalogue of the Richard Owen Collection of Palaeontological and Zoological drawings in the British Museum (Natural History)', in *Bulletin of the British Museum (Natural History), Historical Series*, vol 6, no 5, London, 25 Oct 1979

Lockett, Richard *Samuel Prout*, Batsford/Victoria & Albert Museum (London), 1985

Mills, Christopher (ed), *Images from Nature: Drawings and Paintings from the Library of the Natural History Museum*, The Natural History Museum (London), 1998

Olley, John & Caroline Wilson, 'The Natural History Museum: Alfred Waterhouse' in Dan Cruickshank (ed), *Timeless Architecture,* Architectural Press (London), 1985

Owen, Sir Richard, *A History of British Fossil Mammals and Birds* (London), 1846

Owen, R ed *The Zoology of the Voyage of HMS Beagle under the command of Captain Fitzroy R.N., during the years 1832–1836*, 5 Vols., Smith Elder (London) 1840–3

Owen, The Rev RB, *The Life of Richard Owen*, John Murray (London), 1894

Parker, Sibyl, *Synopsis and Classification of Living Organisms*, II vols, Mc Graw Hill (New York), 1982

Rudwick, Martin JS, *Scenes from Deep Time: Early Pictorial Representations of the Prehistoric World,* University of Chicago Press (Chicago), 1992

Rupke, Nicholas, *Richard Owen, Victorian Naturalist,* Yale University Press (New Haven), 1994

Stearn WT, *Botanical Latin,* David & Charles, (Newton Abbott), 1992

Stearn WT, *The Natural History Museum at South Kensington,* The Natural History Museum (London), 1981

Strickland, HE and AG Melville, *The Dodo and its Kindred or the History, Affinities, and Osteology of the Dodo, Solitaire, and other Extinct Birds of the Island Mauritius, Rodriguez and Bourbon*, Reeve Benham and Reeve (London), 1848.

Sheppard, FW ed Survey of London, Vol XXXVIII, *The Museums Area of South Kensington and Westminster,* Athlone Press, London, 1975

Thackray, John C, *A catalogue of paintings and sculpture at the Natural History Museum London*, Mansell (London),1955.

Yanni, Carla, 'Building Natural History: Construction of nature in British Victorian Architecture and Architectural Theory', University of Pennsylvania PhD thesis, 1994

Yanni, Carla, 'Divine Display or Secular Science: Defining Nature at The Natural History Museum in London' *Journal of the Society of Architectural Historians* Vol.55 No.3, 1996

Yanni, Carla, *Nature's Museums: Victorian Science and the Architecture of Display,* Athlone Press, (London) 1999

This index is devised to allow the reader to refer to all persons, places and institutions named in the text (with the exception of Alfred Waterhouse and The Natural History Museum itself). It also provides reference to the separately named parts of the building, to architectural terms and to materials used (with the exception of terracotta). No reference is made to the individual species drawn by Waterhouse, on the grounds that the text does not attempt to refer to each individually, while the complete list, with reference to the relevant drawings and locations in the Museum, is to be found in the Appendix.

Index